PRAISE FOR

A SLAYING IN THE SUBURBS

"Much more than true crime or another update of *An American Tragedy*. It's an unflinching look inside a marriage and what led to murder." —*Creative Loafing*

"An eventful tale of deceit, jealousy, and the ultimate betrayal . . . [A] good job of filling in the details, fleshing out the scenes, and adding depth by re-creating key conversations of the players." —*True Crime Books Examiner*

Berkley titles by Steve Miller

A SLAYING IN THE SUBURBS
(with Andrea Billups)

GIRL, WANTED

GIRL, WANTED

THE CHASE FOR SARAH PENDER

STEVE MILLER

BERKLEY BOOKS, NEW YORK

THE BERKLEY PUBLISHING GROUP
Published by the Penguin Group
Penguin Group (USA) Inc.
375 Hudson Street, New York, New York 10014, USA

Penguin Group (Canada), 90 Eglinton Avenue East, Suite 700, Toronto, Ontario M4P 2Y3, Canada
(a division of Pearson Penguin Canada Inc.)
Penguin Books Ltd., 80 Strand, London WC2R 0RL, England
Penguin Group Ireland, 25 St. Stephen's Green, Dublin 2, Ireland (a division of Penguin Books Ltd.)
Penguin Group (Australia), 250 Camberwell Road, Camberwell, Victoria 3124, Australia
(a division of Pearson Australia Group Pty. Ltd.)
Penguin Books India Pvt. Ltd., 11 Community Centre, Panchsheel Park, New Delhi—110 017, India
Penguin Group (NZ), 67 Apollo Drive, Rosedale, Auckland 0632, New Zealand
(a division of Pearson New Zealand Ltd.)
Penguin Books (South Africa) (Pty.) Ltd., 24 Sturdee Avenue, Rosebank, Johannesburg 2196,
South Africa

Penguin Books Ltd., Registered Offices: 80 Strand, London WC2R 0RL, England

The publisher does not have any control over and does not assume any responsibility for author or
third-party websites or their content.

GIRL, WANTED

A Berkley Book / published by arrangement with the author

PRINTING HISTORY
Berkley mass-market edition / June 2011

Copyright © 2011 by Steve Miller.
Cover photos: *Girl Running* © iofoto/Shutterstock; *Wanted Poster* courtesy of the U.S. Marshals
Service; *Spring Wood* © Gumenuk Vitalij/Dreamstime.com.
Cover design by Ron Hernandez.
Interior text design by Laura K. Corless.

ISBN: 978-0-425-24034-2

BERKLEY®
Berkley Books are published by The Berkley Publishing Group,
a division of Penguin Group (USA) Inc.,
375 Hudson Street, New York, New York 10014.
BERKLEY® is a registered trademark of Penguin Group (USA) Inc.
The "B" design is a trademark of Penguin Group (USA) Inc.

PRINTED IN THE UNITED STATES OF AMERICA

10 9 8 7 6 5 4 3 2

Most Berkley Books are available at special quantity discounts for bulk purchases for sales, promotions,
premiums, fund-raising, or educational use. Special books, or book excerpts, can also be created to fit
specific needs.

For details, write: Special Markets, The Berkley Publishing Group, 375 Hudson Street, New York, New
York 10014.

To my parents,
Boyd and Julie Miller—they taught me
that words are good friends

AUTHOR'S NOTE

The research for this book was completed with the utmost attention to the truth. Interviews were conducted in cars, in restaurants and bars, in my home office, and in the offices and homes of many of the subjects of this book. Sometimes, someone would call me as I walked down the street, wherever I found myself over the course of a year—Houston, New York, Chicago, Detroit—and I would pull out my pen and go to work on the spot. Some folks don't like to talk, and when they return my call, I take it when and where it happens.

To clarify some of the reporting in this book, a quote attribution that reads "says" means that I, the author, did that interview. The attribution "said" means the quote or statement was derived from other sources, including news accounts, tapes, and letters. Names that have been changed to protect the subjects are noted with an asterisk. This is a

practice I am generally reluctant to do, but I understand
that, in some cases, not doing so would endanger the well-
being of a person, or, in the case of a child, bring to him
or her an undeserved circumstantial notoriety.

Then there are those who made this all happen.

Thanks to Ryan Harmon, an Indiana State Police investigator who worked as hard chasing the subject of this
story as I did telling it. He is a rare combination of learned
and curious cop and a genuine human being. Thanks to
The Berkley Publishing Group for making this my second true crime book for them, and to Shannon Jamieson
Vazquez, Eloise Kinney, and Faith Black. In no order, the
best of the rest include former Marion County prosecutor
Larry Sells, Bonnie Prosser, Kathy Cronley, and Captain
Mark Rice, of the Indianapolis Metropolitan Police Department; Jenna Griffiths and Jon Leiberman from *America's Most Wanted*; and a number of others who agreed to
speak with me on and off the record.

This book was done with the help of a legal reporting
fellowship I received from the Carnegie School of Legal
Reporting at Syracuse University. As a college dropout
and skeptic of higher education, I am nonetheless proud
to be part of that great academic program, which has
proven to impart sound learning for fledgling journalists.
Thanks to Sabrina Lochner, whose help was provided
by the fellowship, for her assistance. Thanks also to
Christian Fuller, a rare combination of friend, lawyer,
and agent.

And most of all, thanks to Andrea Billups, whose un-
wavering support completed this book.

PROLOGUE

Sarah Pender is an affable prisoner, until she speaks. Sitting handcuffed in a Plexiglas booth in an Indiana state penitentiary, wearing her prison scrubs and no makeup, she slides sometimes in her acrylic chair as she speaks and listens. Despite her loquacious nature, she is a very good listener, given to long looks and pensive expressions that convey a pondering of every thought she hears.

But when she talks, it becomes apparent that Sarah Pender is not an average person. She is grammatically correct to a fault—something also notable in her letters, with punctuation that would please any language scholar. And Sarah is also a confident woman who, although she is tethered and unable to walk among us, has no trouble feeling she is your equal.

She often responds to questions with a quizzical look, as if to say, "I can't believe you don't know the answer to that." It is a formidable power play, blatantly condescending, but likely done out of instinct and with no malicious intent.

But there it is.

She was open to meeting with me as soon as I started researching this book, writing me a letter on July 29, 2009, in response to my query and opening with "I wondered when you were going to contact me."

She had already heard about the book, which was good. It meant that the interview process had started. And it's nice to have some word of mouth around the prison, even if its source is unknown.

"Who do you plan on contacting regarding my life?" she asked in that same first letter. "At this time, I don't support that. Just for the record."

As if she had any say whatsoever. Sarah, as usual, somehow believed she had control of this situation and the power to determine how she was portrayed.

"Everyone has a different angle on me, and I'm not into people bothering my family and associates with dumb bullshit."

What she wasn't aware of was what I already knew: her whereabouts during the 136 days of her escape from Rockville Correctional Facility, where she had been serving her eighth year of a one-hundred-and-ten-year sentence for her role in the murder of her two twenty-something roomates in October 2000.

This is something, as I would learn over the next few months, she guarded zealously. It was the subject of her own book, some people told me, which she was at work on when we began meeting in the fall of 2009. The proceeds of that book would allow her to pursue another appeal. At least, that was the plan, her friends said.

My first meeting with Sarah Pender took place at the Indiana Women's Prison, which was in late 2009 located just north of downtown Indianapolis. It was a fine October afternoon, sunny with a firm breeze that told you the quiet of winter was closer than the festivities of summer. The process of getting on Sarah's visitor list was simple and quick—a one-page application, a copy of my driver's license, the approval of Sarah, and I was a certified visitor.

Once I got through security, which consisted of a metal detector, a check of my shoes and socks for hidden contraband, and a light pat down, I was instructed to wait in a short hallway with a few chairs fastened to a bench. The seat placed me in front of a window that afforded a view of what can only be described as a campus, with girls walking alone or in pairs, clad in prison uniforms of varying colors.

If you were to remove the context—a prison with a fence to the outside guarded with weapons—you could imagine this was any women's college. From the inner courtyard, a look at the fencing was out of view, obstructed by redbrick buildings. It was a beautiful campus, in fact.

I was beckoned into the visitation room by a guard. Sarah was ready.

Prisons, both federal and state, generally have two kinds of inmate visitation. A contact visit is one in which the two parties can shake hands, lightly embrace, or otherwise touch. Most prisoners are allowed these, and there is little security risk in a room that is well supervised by guards and monitored via video camera. Then there is the booth visit, in which the visitor sits on one side of a glassed-in booth and the inmate on the other, and the two speak via greasy plastic phone receivers on each respective side of the glass.

The latter is how Sarah meets her public. I was shown to a chair in front of the booth, my back to the room of other visitors, who could hug their incarcerated loved ones. I sat about thirty feet away from those enjoying more personal visits, and although they could hear my end of the confab if they wanted to, visitation at a prison can get loud and almost celebratory, and no one had any interest in the woman behind the glass.

And there sat Sarah, her chair too low, looking small and frail, despite her five feet eight inches height. Once a girl of considerable girth, this Sarah was drawn and, at least physically, defeated. Her pale skin—I had already noticed her fairness in other family pictures—appeared starved for air. She was given one hour a day outside, and despite her reputation and her crime, I felt sorry that she could not enjoy the day that I would be walking into within sixty minutes.

Despite her outward appearance, as soon as she speaks, her undeniable spirit, a somewhat spiritual buoyancy, becomes evident. Robert Hammerle, an Indianapolis lawyer who briefly represented Sarah after she was arrested for murder, was right when he told me, "Say what you will about her, but there ain't no quit in Sarah."

Like her spirit, her steadfastness was also quickly apparent. She is smart and quick to make that known through her speech patterns and references.

Our conversation that day was not unpleasant, but it was guarded. We spoke of some people I had met as part of my research for the book—I had gotten together that morning with a couple of local guys, Leo DeHerdt and John Most, at Carl E. Most & Son, a construction firm that was Sarah's employer at the time of her crime, a crude double homicide in 2000.

"I like John, and I like Leo," Sarah said when I told her they sent their best wishes. She said it in a dreamy breath, almost like she was wishing them there or, more likely, wishing herself back to the damp, cold office she worked in before this all went down.

We talked about her time on the run, and I asked her where she went and what she did. I already knew much of that story but was hoping she might add to some of the information.

"I am writing a book myself," she informed me. "I don't think I want to talk about where I was."

Which was fine, so I changed the subject. Politics? She told me of her admiration for Al Gore and his environmental efforts. She saw *An Inconvenient Truth* as part of a prison class. Food? She enjoyed pumpkin spice lattes at Starbucks. Family? She madly loved her parents and didn't really get along with her sister.

These were things I knew, but my aim was to form a connection of some sort. And she may have known that I knew. Sarah was smart enough not to give up a whole lot. I left the place after the allotted hour feeling good that I had at least created some goodwill and made myself and my intentions known. She was not exactly happy to see someone who would be prying into her life, but she wasn't hostile in any way.

In parting, I told her I had tried to contact Floyd Pennington, an inmate who testified against her at her trial, saying that she had confessed to him that the murders were planned by her and carried out by Richard Hull at her orders. It was some strong testimony and played at least a part in her conviction.

Pennington did some of the state's bidding in eliciting what he described as Sarah's semi-confession. Sarah harbored no small resentment for him, of course. But she almost—almost, I repeat—laughed when I told her about Pennington's two-page letter response to my query. It was a small victory for me to get a chuckle from her.

It also made me realize that relying on inmates and convicts for information is always a hard road. Theirs is a life of deceit, sadly, and I'm sure they feel vindicated for their own dishonesty every time they watch a law enforcement official lie on the stand, which is more common than anyone wants to admit. For the life of a law enforcement agent, too, is one that relies on deceit in order to prevail.

Pennington responded to my letter: "It's no one's business what went on between me and Sarah. She is a beautiful spirit, but so cold emotionally."

He said he was once in love with her, "but she changed

that." Pennington advised that Sarah's road had been a rough one and told me to "leave her the hell alone."

As if all this weren't enough, Pennington said he didn't believe I was a journalist and didn't believe that anyone would write a book about Sarah.

He signed off with a "Fuck off!" and added a cryptic PS—"Her and her sidekick Lynn can both go to hell, I'm no fool."

I have no idea who Lynn is. This is the stuff of lining up inmate interviews.

My second visit with Sarah took place at her new quarters at the former Indianapolis Juvenile Correctional Facility, now the new location of the Indiana Women's Prison. This was a definite downgrade. The prison sits on a hill on the city's northwest side, and the spirit of the place alone was enough to keep one on the straight and narrow. I arrived at around 3:30 on a Monday afternoon in early January 2010, in time to watch a shift change and to be held up by the 4 p.m. inmate count. As I sat there for an hour in the prison lobby, I watched dejected, unhappy prison employees talk about how sad they were the holidays were over and how miserable they were to come back to work every day.

To me, it spoke to the sagging morale that seems to permeate the Indiana Department of Correction (DOC). It is an institution that has seen some very poor performance and doesn't appear to be making any strides toward improving things. Twice in my initial research for this book, an employee of the Indiana DOC hung up on me, literally, when I asked for some help and some access. This is the kind of hostility bred under poor or stressful working conditions. I was hardly discouraged by such conduct; in fact, it created a suspicion that something was very wrong with the inner workings of the system, and they were afraid someone was going to look behind the curtain. That day may yet come.

Finally, at 4:30, Sarah was brought to a visitation cell, the proverbial booth, much like the last one we had convened at, and again we picked up phones, me again looking at the silver handcuffs on her wrists and wondering distractedly if she ever dreamed she was wearing, say, an $85,000 Tiffany scroll bracelet in platinum rather than a $23 pair of Safariland nickel restraints.

I had a list of questions stored in my head. I am not allowed to carry a notepad into the facility because I refuse to go through the media hoops. Instead, I simply appeal to the inmate to get me visiting privileges as a friend.

But my memory is sound, and on this day we started talking, and I fired my queries fairly rapidly. I started with more childhood stuff, moved on to the crime a bit, then danced around her family . . . And then she simply stopped me.

"Listen to you," she said with an easy smile. "It really makes me uneasy being on the receiving end of this interrogation. Can we just have a conversation?"

Of course, I said. A conversation is what good journalists have, sure. Let's do that. She then asked me about myself. How did I become a reporter? Where had I lived?

I actually answered a couple of questions before I realized that she had done it.

Sarah Pender had taken control of the conversation. It was that easy.

Was this how she got people to do her bidding? Is this the ease with which she told her boyfriend, Richard Hull, that their roommates, Andrew Cataldi and Tricia Nordman, needed to be killed? How she earned the love of so many inmates at Rockville Correctional Facility? How she got a forty-one-year-old man named Scott Spitler to toss away a destination job as a prison guard? Or got Jamie Long to give up seven years of her life to cart her away in her prison escape? And, most importantly, is this how she got a successful businessman and entrepreneur—with the help of some of his friends—to stash her away from law enforcement for 136 days after her prison breakout? And how she got the head of a construction firm in Chicago to foot the bill for her apartment in the Rogers Park neighborhood, no questions asked?

Later in our chat, with me now the one on the defense, she mentioned that she was feeling some effects akin to those of Stockholm syndrome. I couldn't get my head around that.

"Do you know what that is?" she asked, eager to be a teacher. I regained my composure.

"No, tell me," I said. I did know, but I wanted her to explain.

She outlined the basics of the affliction, in which prisoners begin to become sympathetic with their captors. She was starting to get along with her guards, she said.

In all, I was amazed as I walked out of the prison. I had been drawn in, manipulated in a fashion. And she really hadn't told me a thing.

I went back to my hotel room that night and began to read through the letters we had exchanged over the past six months. Not a hint of manipulation, but plenty of assertive hubris.

"I don't like thinking of you as an opportunist or someone who would hurt people for your personal gain," she said in a November 8, 2009, letter. "Basically, I was afraid that you would manipulate the information you receive in order to fit your view, or the views of others in positions of power. . . . The filter through which I listen to you and look for you to show up is rooted in a prejudice against [others] and media in general, who created their own version of Sarah Pender."

Responding to interview questions, a letter she wrote dated August 13, 2009, turned the tables. She asked, "Tell me Steve, do you really know why I am in prison? The prosecutor offered three sets, all conflicting accounts, of evidence to the jury.

1. That I did it
2. That Rick did it at my behest
3. That Rick did it and I was just along for the ride

Which one(s) do you plan to present in your book?" These were impressive displays of, shall we say, balls

on the part of a convicted double murderer who was also
lucky to avoid an escape charge. A woman who has to
call a guard to flush her toilet and showers in a cage.

Following that January visit, Sarah sent me another
letter, a continuation of our interview. I had again asked
her what she did while she was free from prison in 2008,
and she came back with this:

"I am sorry to say that you won't have much luck
finding anyone to talk. I led a private, quiet life full of
mundane tasks such as laundry and grocery shopping,
and simple leisure activities like walking in the park and
watching Sunday football. All else is either unknown to
others or private enough to be sort of intellectual property. One should own the exclusive rights to one's own
past and I already feel violated enough. I expect you
might understand this and have some compassion."

I agree with her, of course, and am sickened by our
tabloid culture. But Sarah is a very public person—and
while on the lam, she was a felon whose very past is truly
a public record, and deservedly so—and therefore there
is little compassion for someone who tries to frame the
world to her liking.

Sarah Pender, like so many of those incarcerated,
feels wronged by the system. Her appeals failed, and
Sarah took matters into her own hands. She found a dirty
guard—apparently not a difficult task in the Indiana
DOC—and used him to get her out. She had done her
time, she told everyone. Eight years is long enough, she
said to anyone who would listen.

You've heard about killers and other criminals who

escape prison, reform, and lead exemplary lives ever after until one day, through fluke or fate, they get nabbed and are sent back to prison. This is the story of Sarah Pender, a woman who just about made that break, and she very well could have been your close friend, neighbor, accountant, whatever.

CHAPTER 1

It was the steady *nnnnnnnn* of the eight-cylinder engine that kept her almost calm as she waited to cover the final few feet of her prison escape.

Sarah Pender, a convicted double murderer, lay on the back floor of the idling prison van clad in a blue prison guard uniform. Her partner in the breakout, a hapless guard named Scott Spitler, was smooth talking a colleague, Steven Butler, at the last exit of Rockville Correctional Facility in order to discourage a search of the vehicle. She could slightly hear the murmurs of conversation at the gatehouse ten feet away. But the gentle purr of the engine, mixed with exhaust emitting from the pipes below her, occupied her senses and kept her composed. Sound and smell trumped adrenaline. Sarah shifted slightly, fighting the urge to stick her head up and watch her own plan unfold.

Nnnnnnnnnn, the cylinders pumped. Sarah was this close to ending eight years of incarceration. She had done enough time, she felt. Two years of dreaming and scheming had gotten her to this point. She sold drugs to her fellow inmates, mostly Benadryl, thanks to a web of smuggling that had Spitler delivering the contraband to her in clandestine meetings. The money Sarah made was then sent out to a web of friends outside Rockville, waiting for her to use once she escaped.

She even had sex with Spitler to ensure he was in league with her scheme. She had him wrapped up. If he refused to do anything she wanted at this point, Sarah could simply tell on him and produce the drugs he had brought her, and Spitler's job would be over.

Yes, now, he was doing her bidding. Just as she had planned.

Sarah, at twenty-nine years old, was proud of her ability to organize. A high school honors student, a pre–physics major at Purdue, and intelligence tests that indicated Mensa-level smarts gave her an edge that many said allowed her to manipulate people.

Sarah disputes that vehemently. After all, each person has his or her own will, she argues; along with reasoning, it's a primary mental faculty that separates us from the animals.

But right now she waited while Spitler wrapped up his chat with Butler, the gate guard. He was walking back to the van; she could hear his boots scrape the pavement.

One last gate to pass, and freedom would be in her hands.

As she lay on the floor of the idling van, Sarah was serving her eighth year of a one-hundred-and-ten-year sentence for a double murder. Her prison record held few complaints—she had earned two higher education degrees, sang in the choir, worked on a canine-training program, and enjoyed generally good cheer among her peers and most of the guards.

So it was with some liberty on that sunny summer day, August 4, 2008, that she walked five minutes from her bunk space in a prison dormitory into the facility's recreation room, which offered pool tables, a popcorn machine, weight-training machines, and flat-screen TVs amid potted plants and maroon plastic molded chairs. It was around 2:30 on a normal Monday, a scheduled visit time to the recreational quarters for some inmates. The visits were made on a rotating basis, with one dorm getting access, then another, to avoid crowding.

Once in the rec room, Sarah glanced around and moved quickly to the adjacent gymnasium. The gym, too, was a study in institutional luxury, with a polished wooden floor and basketball hoops that were as new and well maintained as any at the local prep schools, where basketball was the number one sport.

Sarah walked across the empty gym, through a set of gray steel doors, and into a narrow, thirty-foot-long hallway. Under her baggy maroon jail smock and white pants was something she hadn't worn for some time: a set of civilian clothes—a pair of jeans and a plain shirt.

Stripping off her jail clothes, Sarah found an oppor-
tune place to discard them—an open ceiling tile at the
end of the short hallway. Tossing the clothes through the
tile opening, Sarah walked through the next door and
down a one-hundred-foot walkway between an administrative building and an inner security fence, undetectable
to any security cameras.

Although her years of incarceration had put some
weight on her five feet eight frame, she was, at 165 pounds,
slowly striding, as if on air. After she walked past the administrative building, she turned and walked another two
hundred feet past vendors dropping off supplies, a daily
occurrence, and up a sidewalk area through an unmanned
security gate.

She knew the gate would be vacant on a Monday afternoon; Spitler told her so.

The day was magnificent, a blue sky burning high
above the cornfields and soybean patches that lay dream-
ily close now, just down the ridge. And she walked away
from the prison, the sun in her eyes.

Sarah moved through the unguarded gates to a white
Chevrolet extended van that was waiting by the prison's
fueling station. As planned, she crawled in on the pas-
senger side rear doors as Spitler pumped gas on the driver's side, giving her time to slide behind the rear bench
seat of the vehicle.

"When I got into the van, Scott had a prison [guard]
uniform waiting for me to wear so that when I got out of
the van in the parking lot, I would not look suspicious,"
Pender said.

Now wearing a dark-blue short-sleeved shirt, matching pants, and a baseball-style cap, all embossed with a Department of Correction patch, she wedged herself behind the seat and quietly stared at the floor of the van in an effort to contain herself as Spitler headed toward the west gates of the prison, gates that opened into the world that Sarah had missed for nearly a decade.

The fueling area is an enclosure that is entered and departed via gates on each end, the departure gate being the last impediment before leaving prison grounds. Following policy, Spitler stopped the van, got out, and approached the guard at the gate. This procedure is in place to ensure a guard is not acting under duress, such as, well, in the case of an escape. Spitler, though, went a step beyond the procedure and walked to the guard shack and logged the gallons of fuel he had just pumped.

Spitler believed "from previous experience that the guard would not come out and search the van if he walked to the shack," a detective spelled out in an arrest affidavit. Sure enough, the guard failed to come out and look inside.

The gates were opened and Sarah was free. The plan had worked.

But there was one more risk to take. The van edged slowly into the parking lot, where visitors park. Sarah tentatively edged her head up to the window.

"That's my ride right there," she told Spitler.

In the visitor's parking area sat a maroon 1993 Oldsmobile, rusted and dented. Behind the wheel was Jamie Long, a woman Sarah knew briefly as a cell mate in the

Marion County Jail in 2001 and later, over the years, via phone calls, prison visits, and sometimes-passionate letters.

"She's my wife," Long said of Sarah. "We're a lot alike. I'm just another version of her."

Mannish in manner, Long looked older than her forty-two years. Her drinking habit, which landed her in prison for several months at one point in 2004, aged her face to the point where only her deep brown eyes gave a hint of what she once looked like. Her nicotine rasp and light southern accent—leaning more West Virginia than Georgia—combined to make Jamie Long one more Appalachian denizen who had made some tough choices, not all of them good. And while she claimed Sarah as her wife, Jamie was actually married to Larry Long, a handyman and military veteran she had known for over twenty years.

The van pulled up to Long's idling Oldsmobile. Sarah scrambled out and into the front seat of the sedan, and off they drove toward Indianapolis.

"Oh my God, I cannot believe you are here," Long said as Sarah tumbled into the backseat, finding one more change of clothes waiting for her. Spitler drove away, and Sarah quickly stripped off the guard uniform as Long steered down the narrow prison driveway to Strawberry Road, where she headed east toward Rockville, past the Parke County Jail, the Elks Lodge, and and an outpost of the Indiana Army and Air National Guard.

The ride was a glorious tribute to a meticulously

planned reward for Sarah. She had put in place a money-making scheme that utilized her own charisma and organizational skills. She enticed a guard on the inside and an ex-con on the outside to make her freedom a reality.

The roads heading east from Rockville are rolling and smooth, cresting in places to give a panoramic view of the region's gentle landscape.

The two toasted their successful bust out with pulls from a pint of vodka Long had brought along.

"I thought, 'This is an adventure; I can't believe we pulled this off,'" Sarah said. "It was just great."

Their destination was Indianapolis, sixty-eight miles to the east. The two wound through back roads rather than take the direct U.S. Highway 36.

It was a done deal: Sarah Pender, a violent murderer in the eyes of the state, a young woman who had been dubbed "the female Charles Manson," was finally liberated. Her prison sentence was finished, as far as she was concerned. She had often told her friends, "I've served my time," as if hinting at her plans for this day.

───────

Sarah was serving time for the October 24, 2000, shotgun slayings of Andrew Cataldi, twenty-five, and Tricia Nordman, twenty-six, two fugitives from the Nevada Department of Corrections. It was brutal: Cataldi was shot in the chest; Nordman was killed with blasts to the head and chest. The slayers used deer slugs shot from close range, spraying the high-velocity pellets into the bodies and ensuring a messy end. At Cataldi's memorial service, his body was kept on ice because of the large hole in his back from the front-entry gunshot.

Cataldi and Nordman lived with Sarah and her boyfriend, Richard Hull, better known to his numerous friends and acquaintances as Rick or Ricky. Hull was a petty criminal and former high school football star from nearby Noblesville. The four were operating a small drug-dealing ring in the seamy Indianapolis street scene—mostly weed and methamphetamine. Sarah claimed the shootings were committed by Hull, while Hull blamed Sarah.

Sarah rolled the dice with a jury, which found her guilty. She got one hundred and ten years. Hull pleaded guilty and took a ninety-year sentence.

He got hard time, though, in Pendleton Correctional Facility, a tough lockup for hardened criminals. Sarah went to Rockville, which offered some relatively easy time to do, although there were plenty of other women there serving out sentences for violent crimes. The women's prison in Rockville, which held an average of 1,205 inmates a day in 2008, was established in 1970 at a former U.S. Air Force observation base that was built in 1948. It served well as a military outpost, but its turn as a prison was less than sterling in terms of security, with murmurs of corrupt guards and easy contraband. But physically, the medium-security facility, which sits on a hill a mile from a main drag of the Parke County town for which it is named in western Indiana, was beautiful and modern.

Inmates enjoy an atmosphere that is more in keeping with a summer camp than a unit that incarcerates violent murderers. Its staff-to-inmate ratio since becoming a women's prison has been roughly four inmates per guard, average for the Indiana system.

Sarah was typical in that she was there for a serious, violent crime; seventy of the inmates in there with her were doing life, or what would amount to life. But Sarah was encouraged to fit in as best she could and to become part of the facility's community. Women's prisons are vastly different from men's, of course, because gender differences are so vast. Sarah was both a joiner of activities and a leader, sometimes singing for her colleagues.

Few inmates, though, possessed the slick blend of intelligence and street savvy of Sarah; in the land of the blind, the one-eyed man is king. In Rockville, Sarah, despite her involvement in a sordid, horrific crime, was truly outstanding among felons. When she entered the prison system in a state where convicts generally serve one year for every two sentenced, Sarah's first release date was 2055. While in prison, she earned an associate's degree in computer-assisted drawing and a bachelor's in business, giving her time cuts that lowered the date to 2052. It was forever. She wasn't going to wait.

———

If one can plan fate, the escape was an alignment of preordained control.

Sarah Pender had outwitted an entire prison system that is designed to avoid exactly such flights and had done so with a plan so simple, yet flawless, that it took two hours for prison staffers to determine that she was gone. The usual head count at 4 p.m. showed one prisoner short. As according to policy, a second count was done and again showed one inmate short.

At that point, all inmates were ordered back to their dorms for a one-by-one count. It was a top bunk along the south side that was empty in one dormitory: Sarah Pender was gone.

And the caper also had serendipity all over it. Sarah walked past an unmanned security checkpoint. New security cameras were slated to be installed the week after her brazen walkout, cameras that might have caught her in the act. The gate allowing her to meet Spitler was open. The guard at the gate leaving the prison failed to conduct a search of the van in which she was hiding, allowing her to leave the facility grounds. It was a festival of incompetence and corruption, and Sarah was both the leader and beneficiary of the fiasco.

Jamie Long later said that the escape was the product of the perfect storm, a tornadic episode of calculation caused, in terms of timing, by Spitler.

Long said she was told that morning that she was going to have to show up with the getaway car.

"Things were just right," Long said. "From movements that particular day to who was on the gate that day to where he had to be that day, when he'd be back. He called it."

Sarah had more than just good timing and planning going for her. She had also the tight lips of her friends in Rockville, who were well aware of her plot to break out. She also possibly benefited from some bureaucratic in-

eptitude. A Rockville inmate, Sovayda Vasquez, was not
a friend or fan of the popular Sarah. And during the period that Sarah was roping Spitler into her web in order
to enable her to escape, Vasquez was enduring unwanted
sexual advances from a guard, Roger Heitzman, who was
later fired and prosecuted in relation to her complaints.

Vasquez, though, filed a civil rights lawsuit against
the prison system, claiming that it failed to appropri-
ately protect her from Heitzman despite the fact she had
complained.

In her suit, Vasquez also claims that she had warned
prison authorities that Sarah was planning an escape with
the help of Spitler. Nothing was done, though.

And so it was that fate for Sarah was freedom. Knowing that the system's typically loose security would allow
each and every move that day to go unchecked enabled
her plan to unfold. And Sarah was very aware of the lack
of cameras in the facility.

"There was a plan for cameras that was in our goals
and objectives," Pam Ferguson, a prison spokeswoman
says. "The escape by Sarah Pender just sped it up a little.
However, we did have some cameras and we did see
how she got out after the fact. We went back and reviewed. When we knew that the fence had not been
breached, we knew that she didn't go over it, she didn't
go under it, or anything. She had to have gone through a
gate. And as part of the procedures, you start pulling
every tape you have. We did and we saw her come out of
the red building and get into the van, but it was too late
at that point."

The security cameras the prison did have were not continually monitored, another fact that Sarah was bound to know. On the day she walked, there were a couple of cameras that monitored the fence. The plans were in motion to put cameras in every dorm, where they are now.

Sarah escaped on a Monday; a new policy to implement a controlled movement policy was to begin Wednesday. Sarah had all the intel she needed from Scott Spitler.

"It was nothing that was momentarily thought of," said Jerry Newlin, internal affairs investigator at the prison. "There had been quite some extensive time she had put this plan together."

It takes a heck of a planner to unfold something such as this in a place that was supposed to be locked down pretty well.

The security that was planned to be installed was extravagant. In June 2008, orders for more than $250,000 in cameras, cable, mounting supplies, and other hardware were placed. Fiber-optic cable was purchased and ready to be installed in nineteen buildings at Rockville, although it was a task that would take time and was not completed by August. A closed-circuit camera system, at a cost of $294,000, was ordered June 9, 2008, two months before Sarah's getaway in August, and paid for the following January, and was also not in place in August. Sarah watched the work with a wary eye.

Indeed, Sarah had pondered a breakout for about twenty months, mentioning to fellow inmates how easy it would be. Her last appeal had been shot down in 2006, so her indisputable intelligence worked overtime at another avenue for freedom, this one outside the system.

She would occasionally hint to others that she may have a way out. Rick Hull, her former boyfriend and partner in the crime that landed her in prison, was among them. In text messages and occasional phone calls, Sarah advised Hull that she was formulating an escape plan. The two communicated mostly via smuggled cell phones, which were common in Indiana prisons.

"I thought she was blowing smoke, because everyone talks about it and thinks they have it figured out," Hull says. "She had told me at one point that if she got out she would head to Michigan, like she had a plan."

At one point, she told Hull that even if she escaped, "It would blow over."

"I told her then she was crazy and stopped even considering her escape," Hull says. "I told her 'you are a convicted double murderer, and you think if you escape it will just blow over?' She had no idea what kind of thing she was getting into."

But what he didn't know was that Sarah had Spitler under wraps and in her pocket.

"I had no idea she was in with the officer as she was," Hull says. "She had told me something about it, but I just felt that she was being a freak and she's always been a freak. Sure, she'd got an officer on the take. That means cell phones and drugs. But you wouldn't dream of having an officer drive you out."

"I originally had a [guard] uniform of my own," Sarah said. "That's where I got the idea of walking out. It was the gestation of really thinking it was possible. One of my friends worked in the laundry, and we were talking one day, and I said, 'I really gotta get out of this place, I'm escaping.' She asked me, 'How are you going to do that?' and I said, 'I'm just going to walk out of this place because I know how lax they are.' And my friend is like, 'Well, you know, I work in laundry. And in this one back room, they store uniforms. I know they have some jackets.' I was like, 'If I can get some dark pants, I already have my boots and I'm set.'"

Sarah went to work on securing a uniform, volunteering to quilt beds for dogs used in the Indiana Canine Assistance Program, which allows inmates to work with assistant dogs that serve disabled children and adults. Sarah was already a trainer in the program; crafting beds for the dogs was a natural endeavor.

"I thought that I could do a good service and further my plans for escape," Sarah says.

Her notion was to sew a guard uniform into a bed to hide it from the periodic cell searches. Then, at the right time, she would have access to it. But the timing never clicked. OK, she thought, it was just one idea. She waited patiently.

———

When Scott Alan Spitler was hired by the Indiana Department of Correction in May 2003, he was coming off a nearly yearlong stay on disability for an injury he suffered while working as a manager at a local Schwan's food-delivery service.

Spitler, a squat, balding man with a fuzzy draping of facial hair, had turned forty-one the previous May. He was making $881 a week at the time of the escape, according to his personnel file.

The Department of Correction refuses to release any records regarding the escape, including investigations stemming from the breakout or anything the department might have been looking into regarding Spitler's conduct leading up to the escape. But an arrest affidavit for Spitler filed in Parke County three days after Sarah's breakout stated that, according to Newlin, the prison's internal affairs investigator, "Spitler and Pender were already known associates (outside the realm of normal correctional office/offender interactions) prior to this date." Newlin said that "Spitler was also suspected of trafficking and unprofessional conduct with offenders."

And yet, despite suspicion that Spitler was engaging in conduct that could be a security risk, nothing was done to monitor his activities. The assertions from inmate Vasquez never even prompted the smallest concern. Spitler was allowed to carry out his duties without any supervision, an obvious security breach that allowed Sarah to run.

Even Spitler's wife at the time, Rhonda, says that as soon as Spitler began working at the facility, "He started being a jerk." It was a tough job, to be sure, mixing with females who possessed the hardest of street smarts.

The Spitlers had been married for nine years before

the escape. When they wed, she already had five kids and he had two, although many of them were grown and living outside the Spitler home, which sat on a private country road an hour from the prison.

It was a tough marriage from the start, Rhonda says; he cheated on her two weeks after the wedding, she alleges, and things never really straightened out.

As the plot with Sarah intensified, "I thought he was cheating on me again," she says. In fact, Spitler and Sarah had sex only once, maybe twice. The clandestine phone calls Spitler was having were, indeed, with Sarah. But instead of steamy sexual chatter, the talk was of drugs and money.

Spitler told authorities that Sarah promised to pay him $15,000 for helping her escape, and he was pulling in around $300 for a drug drop, taking the goods from the outside to Sarah, who dealt them to inmates.

It wasn't as if guard-inmate sex was an anomaly at Rockville. Kimberly Stull was one of a number of inmates who fell hard for Sarah, and she regarded herself as Sarah's girlfriend for a year of their stay together at Rockville.

Stull, who was released in early 2009 after serving three years for theft and receiving stolen property, says that guards freely exchange sex for favors, such as giving an inmate more free time, removing punishment from inmate files, and allowing drug commerce.

"Spitler was having sex with a couple of girls close to me and Sarah, and we started blocking for him," Stull says. "Blocking" is serving as watch to make sure dalli-

ances go off without anyone getting caught. Closets are
prime territory for these meetings, places where look-
outs can be established and cameras are not present.

"There was a general location for this, in a room off
the gym," Sarah said. Spitler had a key to the room where
chemicals were stored and consequently, the room could
serve as a safe spot for such meetings.

"You could go in there and lock the door from the
inside and do whatever you wanted to do. And we did.
What it told me, with Scott, is that if he's willing to take
this kind of risk . . . he would take another risk. And
that's when I knew he was the man for the job."

Still, male guards having sex with female inmates is
hardly as rampant as the fantasy spun in jailhouse soft-
core movies would have you believe. But in Rockville,
for Sarah, it was a dream scenario.

Spitler, the classic dirty guard, was her foil.

"We owned him, and he fell into the world of dirty
cops, and once that happens, everyone knows and can
get something from them," Stull says. "For Sarah, it all
started with pills, not with sex. Spitler was money hun-
gry, and when we saw that he could bring in whatever we
wanted, it really started. He was bringing in his wife's
pills, Vicodin and Xanax. Benadryl is the hottest pill,
and he was also bringing us that. Cell phones, too, he
brought. At one point, there were three cell phones in
Rockville belonging to me, Sarah, and another girl.
These were the first cell phones ever brought into Rockville, I am pretty sure."

Spitler was bringing them inside in novelty Coca-Cola

cans, which have false bottoms and are just big enough
to hold the phones, which measured about two inches by
five inches, about an inch thick. The power adapters measured about the same size when wrapped up.

Sarah said that Spitler was already bringing in pills,
having sex with the girls, and wasn't really reaping any
great rewards. Sarah said she saw she could provide him
with an incentive—money.

"I simply offered him a business deal. I never black-
mailed him, forced him to bring me in anything or
conned him. I was straight up about our dealings."

The pills came from a number of sources, including
Spitler's own wife. She had been in a car accident in
2002, which put her on disability.

"I didn't like taking pills that much even though I was
in pain," Rhonda Spitler says. "And so I never really paid
much attention to how many were around. I would take
some, maybe get a refill, but right from the start, the doctors gave me a lot."

————

Sarah was found missing shortly after the 4 p.m. head
count. Some inmates snitched on Spitler. He confessed
within twelve hours of the escape and was escorted from
Rockville. As soon as Spitler squealed, the escape hit the
news.

No one at the prison bothered to tell Rhonda Spitler
about the escape and her husband's culpability. She
heard it on the morning news after his arrest.

"The last I ever saw Scott was the afternoon before

[his arrest], when he told me there was an escape at the prison and he had to go in," Rhonda says. "A week later, I met [Rockville prison internal affairs investigator] Jerry Newlin in town to drop off Scott's prison guard uniforms. I filed for divorce later that week."

As Rhonda cleaned out her husband's dresser drawers, among the items was a money order for $200. It was made out to Jamie Long, money that was destined for Sarah to fund her freedom and search for a new life.

"I gave that to the state troopers who were going through the house as part of their investigation. Where it was supposed to go I didn't want any part of it. And I wanted them to find that girl, Sarah."

———

Curiously, the Indiana Department of Correction never felt it necessary to contact the family of the victims nor anyone else who might have ties to Sarah.

The evening of August 4, the day of the escape, a friend in Indiana called Steven Cataldi at his home in Florida. Sarah Pender, the girl who had killed his baby brother, Andrew, had broken out. It was on the news.

"The first thing I thought was 'what kind of prison was she in?'" Cataldi says. "Do people convicted of double murders actually have access to the outside like this?"

He didn't know anything about the country club Rockville had become, where his brother's killer was being kept.

Cataldi's pal said that news reports claimed Pender might head for Florida, where her mother, Bonnie Prosser, lived. Cataldi and his wife, Kathy, lived in Inverness, about seventy-five miles north of Tampa and one hundred and twenty-five miles north of Bradenton, where Prosser was living.

As an ex-military infantryman, Steven Cataldi knew his way around weapons. He pulled his .38 from his office closet and carried it with him, hoping.

"I knew that Pender was supposed to be so smart, went to school to take physics and all that. But I also thought she was stupid enough to come down here. And if she wanted to come by here, I was ready. There would be no questions, no conversation. I would take care of her."

———————

Lauren and Randy Miniaci also lived in Florida, near Bradenton. Sarah had attended the wedding of Randy and her older sister, Jennifer. Randy and Jennifer split up in 2000, and now a somewhat rancorous custody dispute over their daughter, Samantha,* was part of the family fabric. Could Sarah feel the need to reach out, or worse, if she found her way to Florida?

"We sure didn't know, but we kept our doors locked," Lauren says. "I'm still surprised we never heard from the prison system up there."

———————

That's because the system, with a record of flimsy security at a number of its prisons, was doing its best to keep things quiet.

The timing of the escape certainly marred the arrival of Edwin G. Buss, who just three days previously took office as the commissioner of the Indiana Department of Correction.

"It was a terrible embarrassment for him, what a way to start," says one law enforcement official close to the administration. "We were all told that this escapee had to be found quickly and that this [can't] linger. They pulled out all the stops and were ready to spend a lot of money to find Sarah Pender in order to mitigate this humiliating escape."

Buss's office scrambled to spin the episode, though, touting the rapid arrest of Spitler.

"While I am embarrassed for the [Indiana Department of Correction] and deeply angered and disappointed in the officer's conduct that led to the offender's escape, I am proud that my department moved quickly to identify those involved in aiding the escape," Buss's office spat out in a statement. They hadn't even nabbed Jamie Long yet.

Kimberly Stull, Sarah's prison girlfriend, was immediately put into lockdown after the escape and strip-searched daily, mostly as a form of retribution. The guards threatened her, she says. The prison administration knew that she had been somehow helpful in enabling Pender's escape, and that was correct. Still, the contraband trafficking continued.

"Even after Sarah got out, other guards kept doing this," Stull says. "They bring in a bag of pills. The guards select girls they can do this with; they know who won't tell. Sarah knew that, and she used this to get out. She took it one step further than anyone else."

————————

With her head resting on the shoulder of Long, Sarah could not have known what a fury of indignation she had kicked off, nor just how seriously officials took her breakout. All she knew was that the trees looked greener, the vodka had turned to sugar water, and even a ride in a rickety old American car was akin to a limo service.

Perhaps now she could leave her troubling dreams behind, the ones she had endured, the forces of good and evil at war in her head. Sarah had made plenty of friends and enemies during her time in the county jail and in Rockville.

She looked out the window at the world, and she was born anew.

"It was just beautiful," Sarah said.

CHAPTER 2

Sarah Pender liked to throw up. It was part of her bulimia, which she seemed almost proud of.

She said this much after class during her senior year in high school to classmate Barry Wittman as the two walked down a maroon and gray hallway of Lawrence Central High School.

They were headed for a government law group meeting, a group in which they would compete as a part of a regional contest on applications of the Constitution in real-life issues. Heady stuff, to be sure, and Sarah was as smart and engaged as anyone in that class.

Wittman was surprised; he had thought Sarah had outgrown her tendency toward audaciousness and "turned a corner. . . . I was thinking about her in a different way at that time. Then that."

Sarah was the sensible one in whatever group she

became part of as she moved through her last two years of high school, the one who was a fun-loving, jolly care-taker of friends. Although people later in life would say her personality was defined by her remarkable ability to manipulate others, Sarah showed few signs of such a trait as she moved through junior high and high school.

Sarah's mother, Bonnie Prosser, blames her daughter's purging on a household cultivated by a dictatorial father in which Sarah was sometimes the butt of jokes for her weight. Although Bonnie and Roland Pender had split in 1984, the two had an uneasy truce when it came to their children. Visits were as frequent as they could be, given Bonnie's fondness for wintering in warmer climates.

It was during one of their visits in 1997 that Sarah confessed that bulimia might be an issue, although Sarah never admitted it straight up.

"I noticed that as soon as she got done eating, she went to the bathroom," Bonnie says. "She admitted to me that she had thought about making herself throw up. I think it was more than thinking about. I realized also that it had to do with people who were making fun of her weight. Her family made fun of her on the stepmom's side. She was a nerdy, brainy kid who was always put ahead in school."

Sarah's life was one of contradictions. To some, like Wittman, she exposed some of the demons in her life, including her claimed dieting issues, for she had always been rounder than average.

"But she loved to shock people, say things almost

deadpan, and see what the reaction was," Wittman says. "She liked to be the center of attention. And she often was."

He also adds, in noting what would be a sign of things to come, "She was very good at bullshitting."

Plainly put, Sarah, though seemingly well-adjusted, wasn't always honest, and it was hard to know when Sarah was telling a tale. But she told Wittman that she had to be hospitalized at one point because of her bulimia.

"She told me about it, and I think there were some serious issues there," Wittman says. "It's possible she was hospitalized. She missed a lot of school. She was troubled; it was pretty clear to everybody. It wasn't just an eating disorder. There was more, but we didn't know what."

To others, she was a determined, bright, attentive young lady with a good future.

Almost everyone agrees that Sarah Pender was likable, pleasant, friendly, a trifecta of popularity in the high school years as she took her place in the gifted and talented classes. Those classes had a good cross section of kids, some wealthy, some walking the fringes, and some more earthy and altruistic. There was room for everyone. Wittman had the look of a rocker, with long hair and plenty of black clothing. Others were decked in the latest mall fashions.

Sarah Pender's chiseled face has always been more masculine than feminine. She battled weight issues her entire life, her husky, thick-boned frame lending itself to double-digit sizes and loose-fitting band T-shirts and jeans. She wore little makeup or jewelry—"like she was trying not to attract attention at a time when that was the sole aim of most girls," says one friend.

Some of the meaner, less-secure kids made fun of her weight as she grew up. But her intellect fairly dwarfed that of everyone around her. And for that, she was happy.

"She made friends, but sometimes it was hard for them to get along with her because Sarah was always brighter than them," says Bonnie. "So sometimes, it just seemed like she was happier to be on her own or hanging around with her dad or someone older."

Still, a composite portrait of Sarah is a difficult task.

Sarah wore the role of a wise elder well, and many of her friends found her to be a sounding board for their troubles, an older sister who could dispense well-honed advice.

"In our group, she wasn't the one who would always talk, but she was the one people wanted to talk with to get their heads straight," says Joel Walker, who had moved to the school district in 1994 from California. He was the new kid. And almost immediately, Sarah befriended him. In response, Walker developed a crush on Sarah for his entire sophomore year. "Sarah was so much more mature than any of us. It was easy to like her."

She was his friend and somewhat of a mentor to him, turning him on to new bands and letting him tell of his troubles with girls. He never told her of his attraction to her. "Sarah was very plain looking, slightly chunky, but her personality made her very attractive," Walker recalls wistfully. "She had this grace, the ability to talk to anybody, an ability that we were all so lacking at that time in our lives."

They would talk on the phone some evenings, speaking of music, school, people they knew. He told her of himself, of his own life, "but she never talked about herself. I would ask her things, but she avoided them. She avoided home. It seemed like she was always at someone else's house."

Walker had two social outings with Sarah in 1995, red-letter days in his young life, because they were with his beloved Sarah. Too shy to tell her of his attraction to her, he gladly went along when Sarah asked.

"She was the only girl I could talk to," he says. "She was genuinely nice."

One cold February night, Joel's mom drove him and Sarah to Union Station, a small music venue in downtown Indianapolis, to see postgrunge outfit Bush on its first U.S. tour.

"Even my mom said how nice she was. She had this grace; she was the perfect girl to bring home to mom. She always knew what to say."

Shortly after the Bush show, Sarah invited Joel to go bowling, only this time, she had a surprise.

"She brought along a girl, one of her friends, named Ashley, that she was trying to hook me up with," Walker says. "It was a success. I took Ashley to homecoming, and Ashley gave me my first kiss."

But the outing was bittersweet; it was the last time he and Sarah would bond.

"Not only did I have a crush on her, but so did some

of my other friends," Walker says. "She dated a guy, Bill, who was also part of our group. And I was so jealous."

Sarah did give Walker some parting advice, passed along around the time of the bowling outing.

"She told me, 'Don't care what other people think about you. Be yourself.'"

Her spirit of independence was fueled by a legacy of bootstrapping and hard lives lived without fear of being alone. She loved her parents. She worshipped her father, Roland, no matter how hard he was on her.

————————

Roland Pender grew up in Danville, Illinois, in a home that was full of love and reverence for God. One of two boys, he was born in 1953. Roland's mother died when he was an adolescent, and his father, Hugh, a minister, later remarried a woman of faith named Betty Culp, who had three children herself: Tony, Cathy, and Diana.

The families formed a mini Brady Bunch, and the Pender compound consisted of two trailers. In one, the boys stayed, and in the other, the girls lived with their parents.

In 1972, the family picked up and moved to Africa to work as missionaries.

Roland and Tony refused to go. Tony left for California to live with his birth father.

Roland was by that time old enough to stay in Illinois and forge for himself. He was a self-taught type, good with his hands and a prolific partier who paired his long hair with bib overalls.

"Our whole family bounced around, all over the country, and the world," says Tony Culp, Roland's half brother and Sarah's uncle. "Because of that, we weren't real close, but we always got along well when everyone was together."

Culp is three years younger than Roland, and he looked to Roland and his pioneering spirit as inspiration over the years. Even in his teens, Roland was handy, starting one job as a draftsman, then doing machine maintenance, and moving on to plumbing and electricity.

"You see quickly where Sarah got her smarts," Culp says. "Roland doesn't talk much but he can really understand very complex things. And he doesn't let on; he just does it."

Roland soon got a good-paying job as a truck driver, hauling fish from breeding farms and hatcheries into processing factories. He was making friends as he figured out how to make his mark in the world. Among those friends were fellow truck driver Don Neice and his wife, Carol. Roland and Don were fishing buddies. Once in a while, the bachelor Roland would come over for a home-cooked meal.

———

Bonnie Wagner was born in Erie, Pennsylvania, in 1956 to Mary Ella and Lawrence Wagner. Her mother was a dietician at the local hospital, and her father worked at LORD Corporation making airplane parts.

The youngest in a brood of three girls and a boy,

Bonnie was part of a nomadic tribe. Her mother "was a strange gypsy woman," Bonnie says.

"To this day I do not know why she was always so antsy about moving," she says. From Erie, the family moved to Tucson, Arizona, in 1966, then to Southern California, then to rural Funston, Georgia, near the Florida border. Sometimes her father would accompany them, and other times he would stay in California taking care of his aging parents.

"My mother and father never split up, but he would come to us to help us when we moved, then go back to California," Bonnie says.

When Mary Ella took the family to Phoenix, Bonnie was sixteen and decided to stay, even when the next trek was to California for the rest of the Wagner clan. She had seen enough of the road for a while and was burned out on it early in her life.

Bonnie worked for a handicapped woman through an arrangement with a local church, assisting her with day-to-day chores and errands. It was hardly the life for a teenager who had never spent more than three years in the same place during her brief life.

"I was lonely, I needed some kind of family, and I didn't want to go back to moving everywhere," Bonnie says. "I couldn't handle just being there in Phoenix and having no friends or anything."

One of her sisters, Carol, lived in Greencastle, Indiana, with her husband, Don. They had a friend they thought Bonnie might like.

"Would you like to meet him?" Carol asked Bonnie.

It was 1976, and Bonnie was nineteen years old and restless in one more new place. The very ambitious Roland Pender was just the antidote for her restlessness.

They met over dinner with Carol and Don and began dating almost immediately. Roland was easy to like, simple but with a dash of intense intelligence that transcended his truck-driving occupation. He didn't just want to deliver fish; he wanted to know how the whole process worked.

One day, Roland was getting ready for another run, and Bonnie was in a hurry getting ready for a job interview. There was a waitress job open at local diner. But Roland saved her.

"Why don't you forget the interview and come with me?" Roland said.

She thought he would never ask. She climbed aboard the truck and into Roland's life.

The two became a team, moving from the lakes on down to Arkansas, where the fish were sliced, diced, and frozen for distribution to restaurants all over the south.

"Hot weather, stinky fish," Bonnie recalls. "It was great, interesting work."

When the rest of the Pender family returned from Africa, Roland and Bonnie were married and had a child, Jennifer, who was born in 1977.

The idea that they would get married startled Tony Culp, who returned to Illinois to greet his family. The 1970s were winding down and still had the freedom-embracing hangover induced by the swinging 1960s. Marriage was hardly at the top of the priority list for many young people.

"I was surprised when I met Bonnie," he says. "She was a bit plain but really nice, and I could see why he would be with her. She was very sweet and very kind. But at that time, people just weren't getting married at such a young age."

But the family immediately embraced Bonnie, who had sought stability for so long.

Diana, in particular, loved Bonnie. "Bonnie, she was a very good person. I still have pictures of her swinging on a swing set one day. It was about a year before Sarah was born."

Sarah Jo Pender was born on May 29, 1979, the youngest of two daughters born of Bonnie and Roland. The family lived in Greencastle, Indiana, where Roland now worked at Economation, a conveyor-belt company. Bonnie, having been in one place for almost three years straight, was content to be a housewife. She always could handle kids, who liked her intuitively. And although her own were a challenge, she loved doting on them both.

Sarah's sister, Jennifer, was the rebellious one, a troubled, loud, and abrasive child who could never be completely calm. Sarah was serene from the start, a blissful, smiling baby who curiously loved life.

Both girls were held to high standards by the strict Roland, right from the start. His approach to parenting conflicted directly with Bonnie's. She tended to be a more hands-off, "let kids be kids" parent, whereas Roland ruled with discipline at the center of his conduct.

As the two children grew, the parenting conflicts became more and more contentious.

It began to infiltrate the marriage, Bonnie says, in that Roland expected the same excellence from Bonnie as he tried to pull from his children.

"Nothing was ever good enough," Bonnie says. By now, Roland was learning the conveyor-belt business at Economation from the inside out. He was learning drafting and reading blueprints, on the fast track to some kind of management position. He was traveling around to service the company's wares. The Budweiser brewery in Milwaukee used them. It was a huge account, and the work got Roland acquainted with some of the bigger business names in the region. In the future, he would make quite a bit of money as founder of his own company, Integrated Conveyors.

But before he could do that, he and Bonnie got a divorce in 1984.

"He got an attorney to draw it up, and I signed the papers the next day," Bonnie recalls. "It was short and sweet."

Bonnie left Indiana in January 1985. Sarah was five. Most in the family didn't know the reasons, which is the way it should be.

"I really don't know why she left, but I suppose she had her own issues," Diana, Roland's half sister, says. "Roland would never talk about it."

Bonnie's reasons for the demise of her marriage and her departure range from the stifling atmosphere under the thumb of Roland to the ailing health of her father, who was now living in Anaheim, California.

"It was not an easy decision," Bonnie says. "I could not afford to keep the house we had in Indiana, it was a new three-bedroom brick place, and also take care of family. Roland had a good job, and so I went without the children. And I knew the kids had a good home to be in."

Roland took full custody of the girls and lived as a single parent, quickly earning the admiration of his family and friends.

Bonnie stayed in California for a while, living in a tent for some time, again lost and adrift. She came back to the Greencastle area in 1986 and began to have regular visitation with her children. Over the years, she would wed three more times for periods ranging from one to thirteen years.

Roland, meanwhile, met his next wife, Sheryl, in the early 1990s, and the two got married shortly thereafter and soon moved to a home in northeast Indianapolis.

———

Despite having both birth parents within a one-hundred-mile radius, the Pender home was broken in the strongest figurative sense; it was a merry-go-round of custody in which no one was ever quite satisfied.

An investigation into Sarah's background would later find, inconclusively, that Sarah "claims her stepfather sexually abused her," although the claim was never substantiated with police reports or any other kind of authoritative confirmation. Sarah would repeat it to friends over the years, even at some points blaming her drinking and drugging on her "background" and asserting in communication with others that she understood the pain of molestation.

Even today, she asserts that she is "part gay," with a tinge of remorse not at her sexuality but at the reaction to the notion.

"Maybe I wouldn't be if my stepfather hadn't molested me at age nine," Sarah says now.

This episode, which occurred during a short-lived marriage between Bonnie and a man named Jack,* was never made known to Bonnie until much later, after the girls were both grown and out of the home.

"Jennifer initially told me that Jack had tried it with her and didn't succeed," Bonnie says. "Sarah told me in 1999. She said that he had Sarah try on my negligees. To this day, I am not sure how far it went. But I know that for a long time, Sarah thought it was her fault. I think it did cause her great problems over the years. She was really confused about men. She was looking for someone to love her."

Jack and Bonnie divorced, and Bonnie spent some time on her own. A year later, when Sarah was ten, Jennifer went to live with Bonnie while Sarah stayed with their father. Then at age twelve, in 1991, Sarah also went to live with Bonnie, who had remarried and was living outside Indianapolis.

The next year, as she entered junior high school,

Sarah was back living with Roland and her stepmother for an arrangement that lasted through her high school graduation. She missed her real mother, and Sarah visited Bonnie on weekends, summers, and holidays.

Despite their shared tumultuous upbringing, Jennifer and Sarah were never close, with a relationship that was both competitive and rancorous.

As the years passed, it became apparent to others that Jennifer was the favored daughter in Roland Pender's home.

"I saw a lot of favoritism," says Diana, one of Sarah's aunts. "Sarah was happy on the outside, but as she got older, it seemed like she was kind of presenting that only. She never gave much of herself away. Deep down she wasn't happy but instead tried to please others. When she was little, she smiled all the time and had this great personality."

The family on Roland's side would have outings—camping, fishing, walking in the woods. One year, when Sarah was in her early teens, she and Diana and some other family members went wading in a creek near the campsite.

"Sarah lost one of her Birkenstocks," Diana recalls. "She thought it was funny; she looked and looked in the water. She wasn't disturbed at all. She just said she was afraid her dad would be mad."

Sarah never seemed truly at ease in her father's house. Sarah was not happy having a stepparent, Diana adds. To compound that, Jennifer was thin and pretty, while

Sarah's weight was indelicately dealt with. Jennifer was always the priority.

Predictably, amid festering resentment, the Pender girls battled.

"She was absorbed in her life and was too busy to be bothered with me unless she was recruiting me to use as an alibi for some sort of late-night trouble," Sarah says. "In high school, we never mingled, shared no friends, and never attended the same functions. . . . There were rare moments of unity but they were fleeting and generally hinged on loathing our parents. . . . At least when Jeni was around, I had a little backup when it came to us [against] them, as with any stepfamily experiences.

"Even though she came to live at Dad's her last two years, we didn't grow close despite sharing a room. With a two-and-a-half-year age gap, I was an annoying little sister, ripe to be made fun of, and she had our stepsister, the same age as her, to team up with. The only things my sister taught me were how to tease my hair, sneak out late at night, and properly unroll a condom."

Jennifer was the fashionable one, into the latest styles. Sarah was cerebral, into friends, music, and anything that got her out of the house.

"And when she left, I was fifteen and left to fend for myself inside a family, school, city, and life that I never felt like I belonged in."

Getting a B on a report card meant some punishment at home, usually a grounding. But Sarah was also taught household duties, and she could set a dining table with fastidious detail.

One night, her mother, Bonnie, came and picked up Sarah, at that time in junior high, to take her to dinner, a girls' night out. As soon as they were seated, Sarah began to tidy the table, straightening the silverware and napkins.

"What are you doing? This is a restaurant," Bonnie said.

"This is what we do at home; everything should be set up right, and they have it wrong here," Sarah said.

It was a stringent life in the Pender home. And if the rigid discipline was not enough, Sarah also suffered the usual indignities at the hands of her older sister.

"I was routinely made aware of every flaw I ever dreamed of having," Sarah says, still sensitive to criticisms that almost every sibling engages in.

But the years were kind to Sarah in at least one sense; her academic achievements mounted. Although her weight issues presented the usual youthful trauma, her brainpower gave her an identity.

Realizing her strong suit, Sarah became a joiner: a week at Hanging Rock Christian Academy in fourth grade, a term in the Business Basics program of Junior Achievement in sixth grade, and the choir at Belzer Middle School in seventh grade.

In 1992, she received a letter of commendation from Indiana state representative Brian Bosma hailing her "superior academic performance" and placement on the honor roll with distinction at Belzer. On her seventh-grade College Board tests, Sarah placed in the upper 12 percent for language arts.

Sarah took a Safe Sitter seminar at age eleven and babysat for neighbors, earning money to spend on the music she was growing to love. She mowed lawns and filled in at her father's business doing filing work. As she grew into a teenager, Sarah took turns working at Kroger, Steak 'n Shake, Big Boy: "I worked summers and weekends during the school year, as much as my work permit allowed me," she says. "My father instilled a strong work ethic in me. As long as I can remember, he worked hard and taught me that working was a responsibility."

She also sang in the local United Methodist church choir for a year, where she made a number of new friends.

"She was bubbly and high energy," says Teresa Walters, whose husband was pastor of the church. "She had a lovely voice. She was a popular girl."

Then there were those demons . . .

———————

"At 15, treated on an inpatient basis at Community North for depression, then had group therapy at Gallahue," a mental-health facility, reads a report on Sarah, coldly analytical. The analysis is part of a presentence document that would come much later.

The depression was diagnosed by a family doctor after being told that Sarah was not doing her household chores and not paying attention to what she was told to do.

"In other words, she was a normal adolescent," says

Bonnie, who found out that Sarah was being given Prozac during a routine visit one weekend. Bonnie blames the diagnoses on confused parenting at the Pender home; a kid who doesn't do what she is told is not necessarily depressed.

"She told me she had to take one of her pills, and I said, 'What pills?' I had no idea she was on anything."

After Sarah handed her mother the pill bottle, Bonnie promptly jumped in the car and drove to the nearby pharmacy.

"Can you give me some literature on this drug," Bonnie asked the pharmacist. He handed her the three-foot-long explanation of the controversial drug.

"I freaked out," Bonnie says. A small battle between her, Roland, and Sheryl ensued, won by Bonnie. No more Prozac. But the inpatient treatment would continue, she allowed.

Sarah went to therapy to deal with abandonment issues, Bonnie says. Leaving her and returning to Roland's home after that year during sixth grade bothered her and could probably be partly the reason for her recalcitrance at home with her father and stepmother.

Bonnie attended some of the therapy at Gallahue, even going to the facility when Sarah was evaluated.

"I had to tell them that while Sheryl may not have thought Sarah was acting 'normal,' whatever that is, what's normal for one person is not normal for another," Bonnie says. It was a battle to keep Sarah away from the psychobabble advocates, she says, and she is satisfied that they never did any damage to her Sarah. But there was more at play than just the struggle over some form of treatment for a somewhat vague malady.

Friends and acquaintances saw that there was more going on with Sarah in high school than church choir and upper-level academics. Her popularity gave her an in with a number of elements, not all of them good.

"She was one of those people that everyone liked," one former classmate says. "She just had that personality that made her get lots of friends. It seemed as if she wasn't home often, just out with friends all night. Junior and senior year I saw less and less of her. The word going around was that she was starting to get deep into drugs, and I believed it because a few of her friends were well-known drug users. . . . [Still], she was one of the nicest, friendliest people I've ever met."

Another classmate, who had attended middle school with Sarah, left, and then returned in tenth grade, says Sarah had changed. "She had a reputation for sleeping around," he says. Like her classmates, she had also matured somewhat and now had access to drugs and alcohol.

Sarah was walking on both sides of the fence in terms of her high school life. On one side of that fence was a studious but somewhat bohemian crew; this was the gang that came to her house on her sixteenth birthday and gave her a copy of Stone Temple Pilots' *Purple* CD before sitting down to watch the horror flick *The Dark Half*. And when it came to academic exercises, Sarah was very comfortable with her high-achieving friends. She took the role of George Eliot in a classroom exercise titled "Meeting of the Minds," adroitly handling the part of the female natural-law thinker and novelist.

There was still the other side, though, the older batch of kids who were no doubt headed for bad things and worse places. Sarah found herself in the middle.

"Sarah lived in two worlds," says classmate Taylor Walters. "She was in honors classes, sang in the school's show choir, and was active in the church youth group. She also [took drugs] and engaged in a lot of sexual experimentation at a young age. I never viewed her as a mean or violent person—just self-destructive."

The trouble was continuing to show up at home, as well. When she was sixteen and before she got her driver's license, Sarah stole her stepsister Megan's car. When the car ran out of gas not far from the family's home in northeast Indianapolis, Sarah returned to the house and took her stepmother's car, which contained some expensive jewelry and cameras. As she made a hurried escape, not more than three miles from the house, Sarah ran a light and was struck broadside by another car. Her injuries included a broken pelvis and a police record for taking the car. She was in a wheelchair for months. Counseling, court dates, a short stay in a juvenile home for girls, and deferred adjudication followed.

Bonnie came to visit her daughter one day at the girls' school, supporting her upcoming release. She was unprepared when Sarah pulled a letter from the shelf of her room at the institution and began to read it to her.

"You left me and left your responsibility," Sarah read, the letter being part of an exercise given to her as part of her counseling. To Bonnie, it sounded like a somewhat rote excuse for misbehaving. But she swallowed and listened.

"You never took care of me and acted like I was not there," Sarah continued. But Bonnie had heard enough.

"Your dad took a lot of responsibility away from me," Bonnie told her. Although there was little she could say to excuse deserting the family, at least she knew she'd had good intentions in her heart.

Sarah was released after a few weeks, but the scars remained. She was resolute, though, in continuing to do her best in school and achieved the highest levels she could. Still, she had a tendency for self-destructive ways and found that she could get the attention she so wanted by saying outrageous things and, sometimes, committing outrageous acts like stealing a car.

The yin-yang societal worlds Sarah cultivated stemmed from a passionate desire for acceptance, mother Bonnie says. "She did not know which place she fit and at the same time she wanted to find out something about everyone," Bonnie says. "She might go to a church function one night and out with some dope-smoking friends the next night. I just told her, 'Please be careful who you are with and don't trust people until you really know them.' Sarah was very trusting, and as she moved through her teenage years, she was teetering on which side to fall on."

Still, Sarah finished high school in 1997 with a flourish, a popular girl who had managed to get some of her wild habits under control and was looking forward to college.

Seventy-five percent of students that graduated Lawrence Central that year went to college, compared to around 67 percent nationally, according to the National Center for Higher Education Management Systems.

Sarah's father, Roland, encouraged her to go to college. She finished high school with a 2.6 grade-point average, hardly the rank of a studious academic. But she achieved a milestone when she was accepted at Purdue University and enrolled as a pre–physics major. Her dad had agreed to foot the bill for the year.

During the summer before she left for Purdue, Sarah worked three jobs to save money for her expenses while attending college; she sold software, books, and music at a retailer; cashiered at a local grocery store; and tested products for an engineering firm. She had her head in the game, despite the constant tug of the party life. She had her sharp, fertile mind and a father who was willing to make her academic dreams come true. She also had David, a boy who attended a nearby high school. The two dated during Sarah's last two years in high school as she worked to keep away from bad influences and older kids. While he wasn't the brightest or most ambitious guy, they shared a love of music and Sarah was somewhat serious about him.

It was a tough year for Sarah in West Lafayette, Indiana, where Purdue's forty-thousand-strong student body takes up most of the town. The town overlooks the Wabash River, which runs to the north and south of the town, about an hour's drive west of her dad's home. Sarah started the academic year in fall 1997 with promise, achieving some decent grades and living in a dorm, but she quickly slid as she discovered the bars of the Wabash Riverfront District and the party life of a college town.

The weed was pulling Sarah into a new world, one in which intelligence was considered rare and where earthly pleasures trumped spiritual and intellectual ones.

Her lifestyle was a standing contradiction as she wound her way through the Purdue system her freshman year. She was circumspect and studious at times, and profligate at others.

"By my second semester, I was too interested in parties, drugs, and men to do my homework or attend lectures," Sarah says.

Her mother had urged her to take some time off, to enjoy being a young lady before embarking on a career path. But her father would not hear of it.

"I thought it was awfully hard on her to get right out of high school and into college without any time for herself," Bonnie says. "She was taking trigonometry and a number of other hard classes in her major. And she just got burned out. She started partying with her friends and her grades started to drop."

"I regret going straight from high school to college," Sarah says. "I needed a year to experience freedom, as I had too little of it at home growing up. I always felt like I was a step behind everyone else, like they were busy living life and I was busy trying to figure out what was going on."

Following the first semester of college, Sarah came

home triumphant at having made it through with some decent grades in some hard classes.

But something was wrong; she was developing a taste for more subversive activities. Although sex had played a role in her life from the start of puberty, Sarah's tastes were developing.

She paid a visit to Lawrence Central High School shortly before Christmas that year, visiting some of her favorite teachers and saying hi to administrators.

"But it seemed that something was wrong," says Jason Newsome,* who was the instructor of a government class and an academic team on which Sarah had been a leader. "She came to my room after school, and she started telling me about Purdue and how she liked ordering her boyfriend around and how she was getting into S and M. We had never had the kind of relationship where she should be talking with me about this stuff."

Newsome felt the discomfort level rise in the room with just the two of them alone. It was Sarah's stock-in-trade more fully developed. She was shocking. But Newsome got an even creepier feeling that she was telling him the truth, a truth that he wanted no part of.

"This was a guy she was going out with at Purdue, and I got the feeling that she liked having power over this guy," Newsome says.

At the same time Sarah was feeding the seedier elements in her life, she also maintained the calmer, more considered side. David, her high school boyfriend, was the anchor to that for the time being.

"He shared my desire to walk the straight line," Sarah

says. "In order to stay out of trouble [during points of high school], I ditched almost all of my friends, didn't go to parties or functions much, and focused on school and work."

Even through college, she stayed with David, for the most part.

"We were likely the only sober people at concerts like Ozzfest—we saw the reunion of Black Sabbath—X-Fest, and a host of other major rock events.

"When I got to college, I focused on school and fostering new relationships with people," Sarah says. She stayed in an all-girls dorm known to fellow students as the "Virgin Vault." She had a 7 a.m. calculus recitation class, which was just a start. In her freshman year, she also took physics, chemistry, psychology, and French.

David came to visit nearly every weekend. She wasn't truly in love, but he was a partner with whom she had a history.

So when the school year at Purdue ended, so did Sarah's college career. It was time to get a job, goof off, see concerts, get high.

She and David got a place to share, a two-bedroom town house. They took a roommate, Sarah got a job as a cashier at a grocery store, and David worked sporadically as a landscaper, roofer, window washer—whatever he could find, if he could find it.

"And when he wasn't working, he didn't do much more than sit around and play video games," Sarah says.

One day, she quit the grocery store with nothing else to fall back on, instead pawning some of her possessions and taking on the shiftless life that kids do when they just aren't sure what the future holds.

————————

She was running out of affection for David, who was by now content to sit home, play video games, and let the world go by. Sarah also had that wild streak that would not relent. She landed a job at Carl E. Most & Son, a construction firm located on the south side of Indianapolis. The fifty-five-year-old firm was a midsize company that did midsize projects, things like revamping ailing industrial buildings. It was an enterprise that gave the company lots of business, and by the time Sarah joined the administrative office staff, Most & Son was billing out $3 million a year with a staff of about thirty.

Sarah was proficient in a profound fashion; days after hiring into Most at $10 an hour, she was charged with writing professional correspondence with the company's vendors. Her pay increased as her skill developed, and she discovered she had an uncanny aptitude for doing clerical tasks like managing payroll, bookkeeping, creating job estimates, and reading blueprints.

"I was [also] getting the itch to party, and Dave just wasn't the social type. I met a lot of guys who promised more than what Dave was giving me, so I broke it off with Dave before I was tempted to cheat," Sarah said.

When she did break it off, David trashed the town house—"I really couldn't do much, so I sat back, smoked a fat-ass joint, and watched him go about doing his thing," she said.

Over the years, Sarah would think about David and do the "what-if?" pondering, even wondering out loud to her mother, Bonnie.

"She says to me sometimes that she wishes she had stayed with him," Bonnie says.

In 2005, Sarah wrote a letter to David, outlining her remorse over not sticking with him. She spoke of an unwanted pregnancy, with him as the father; an ensuing abortion of that baby; and a wrong turn that landed her in prison.

"After five years of pain and trouble, of empty and shallow love," Sarah said, "I should've stuck it out."

————

But post-David, officially ensconced in the workaday world, Sarah was pulling an eight-to-five shift five days a week and using her weekends for getting stoned and partying with friends. She took a small apartment on the city's north side, on Governor's Court, not a great neighborhood but something that fit into her budget.

Soon enough, she was earning $12 an hour and taking home $212 and change every week. For a nineteen-year-old, she was keeping her own place, working a decent job, and driving a car her father had helped her buy. It wasn't going to be enough to keep her life afloat. The specter of more college always loomed, and Sarah never counted herself out of that for the future. It was now, though, that she wanted to enjoy.

She was like millions of other late teens and twenty-somethings all over the world. She was finding herself.

Sarah fell into more drugs. In late 1999, she met a welder—blue-collar types were often around the Most offices—who had access to high-grade cocaine, and he and Sarah became "coke-sniffing fuck buddies," she said. "I began buying almost an eight-ball a week."

Still, just as in high school, Sarah managed to walk in two worlds. She and her mother were growing closer, even as Sarah's predilection for the wild life was slowly taking over.

In the fall of 1999, Sarah had moved to a nicer neighborhood on the northwest side, a developing community with tree-lined streets and a benign family atmosphere.

"This was the nicest place, and a time that Sarah and I were very close," Bonnie recalls. "It was a one-bedroom lower level with a patio, and it was Christmastime. We decorated the place so nice, and it was everything I had dreamed of for her. We baked cookies, I remember, to celebrate her new place."

That fall, Sarah also changed jobs, working with national accounting firm Crowe Chizek—now Crowe Horwath—through a temporary agency. It was one more opportunity for Sarah to use her developing accounting skills, which were primarily learned through some self-motivated teaching and a couple of classes in high school. Sarah's sense of order made the occupation a natural fit for her.

CHAPTER 3

The partying became relentless in the first half of 2000. She was robbed of some acid she was trying to sell. She was mugged on the street. She was raped by an acquaintance the week prior to Easter in 2000.

Sarah and a male friend had met at another friend's house on the south side. The person who lived there was named Jesse Kutcher, and Sarah and he knew each other through a number of mutual friends.

It was a weeknight, and Sarah had had enough to drink and was preparing to leave with her friend. But Jesse urged her to stay and have a couple more. She relented. A big mistake.

"Sarah was supposed to come over the next night, but she called and asked if we could make another plan a couple of days later," Bonnie says. It was Easter weekend and the two got together Saturday.

"Sarah was wearing a sweatshirt that kind of covered her up," Bonnie recalls. "But I saw bruises on her arms and I asked her about it."

"Mom, I have to tell you," Sarah said. "I was attacked by this guy."

"You better tell me who it is," Bonnie demanded.

"I can't," Sarah said. She did not tell until years later. Jesse continued to bother Sarah over the next few months.

Her living was hard and what some might consider dangerous, filled with strangers of dubious character. She and her friends were "steady going out to the bars and clubs picking up guys in pairs," Sarah said.

The risks pursuant to that lifestyle were plain. Sarah now lived in a world in which criminals and street characters were the main inhabitants. Her rape was never brought to the attention of the cops. Her mugging never resulted in a prosecution. The streets are indeed mean, and Sarah was now part of them.

Even then, though, Sarah found time to be there for her family. When her grandfather Hugh, Roland's father, died, Sarah shuttled back and forth between Indianapolis and Westville, Illinois, ninety miles, to help her grandmother Betty ease into widowhood. "We all helped out, but Sarah was really a presence," said Tony Culp, her uncle. "She was there a lot and she was always bubbly and so kind to her grandmother."

Sarah continued to be employed by Crowe through May 2000, when she returned to Carl E. Most & Son. It was home for her, a messy place filled with rough-hewn folks who worked hard building jobs. The place was run

now by John Most, son of Carl, and John was both mirth-
ful and coarse. Sarah became his confidant and handler,
someone John looked to for organization in his daily
affairs.

"Nothing bothered her; she had this mentality that
was both serious and fun," Most says. "She was also just
this close to crazy. I used to scream at her when she
would get a new tattoo, and I would chew her out for
staying out late playing pool with her boyfriends."

"Sarah loved to shock us," says Leo DeHerdt, controller at Most. "She'd say, 'Leo, you wouldn't believe the
things I do at night.' So I'd ask her, 'What are we talking,
whips and chains?' She'd just say, 'You don't want to
know.'"

Changing clothes in the parking lot, which was on a
main thoroughfare in the city's industrial area, was standard for Sarah. Her sense of humor, again, served her
well and made everyone around her feel at ease.

"We'd hear cars honking and all of this, and there she
would be, outside, putting on a new top or something,"
Most recalls.

One day, out of the blue, Sarah brought in a new friend,
a girlfriend, clad in a red robe and fuzzy red bedroom
slippers.

"And she said, 'This is my bitch,'" Most recalled.
"And she gave her a big kiss—smooch. We were im-
pressed."

Most of this sort of display was intended to entertain John and the rest of the crew at Most. The girl was
Stephanie Slocum, just one of her friends.

"She was heterosexual. It was a joke," Sarah says. She loved the shock value of such stunts.

Her employment was the one constant in her life, which was starting to get a bit out of control. Her partying ways, various boyfriends, and hedonistic tendencies were taking over. Although she was staying clear of the law, she was also walking with a wilder crowd, where drugs were the center of the action.

———

On July 11, 2000, the jam band Phish sat at the top of the heap among touring rock acts. The band's tours drew followers from all over the country, and the Grateful Dead vibe created legions of Phish-heads, who faithfully followed the band everywhere. Sarah couldn't do that, of course; she was responsible enough to keep a job and a steady income.

But she could certainly head out to the show at the Deer Creek Amphitheater in nearby Noblesville that night. It would be the start of a long, fateful turn.

"There was a house across from Deer Creek where the party never stopped," says Brian Harrison, whose high school friend, Rick Hull, was a former star athlete in high school but had, at that point, turned his life over to intoxicants of any strain. Hull had been to rehab twice, Harrison says, but it didn't take. He was an acid-tinged, pot-smoking, hard-drinking man whose primary job was selling drugs, which he augmented with sporadic turns as a bouncer at any club that would have him.

That day, before the Phish show, Harrison says,

"There was a pool at the house, and we were having a party, and Sarah was at that party with a couple of friends."

―――――――

Richard Hull was born November 4, 1977. His storied legacy as a high school football tackle, both offensive and defensive, remained intact in his hometown, as did his strong family ties.

One of three children, Rick was raised by his mother and grandmother in a pale-green wood-frame house on Clinton Street, a redbrick-paved avenue in the older part of Noblesville, a growing and upscale town that was becoming an extension of Indianapolis. Rick's father and mother split when Rick was four, and Rick initially spent some weekends with his dad, but it didn't last. The elder Hull was a tanker and spent more time in Florida, unloading boats, than in Indiana.

Rick grew up fatherless, he says. To replace that masculine presence in his life, he embraced a masculine pastime: sports. He was wrestling competitively at the age of six and moved into football at the same time.

"The first time I ever saw my mom cry was when I was wrestling at a tournament and all the other kids had their dads there," Hull says. "And I asked her where mine was."

Rick's mother, Debbie, worked as many as three jobs at a time to make her way—running the cash register at Dairy Queen, working the counter at a pizza place, or folding clothes at a Laundromat, anything that would pay the bills and take care of everyone. Rick's sister, Tabitha, was five years younger, and a stepbrother, Ronnie Penwell, was four years older and rarely present. Like many kids, Rick's love of sports provided him a platform for his competitive nature and gave him a social appeal that the otherwise shy boy might not have been granted.

"He played everything, you name it," Tabitha says. "Baseball, football, basketball, track. And he was big, always. He was ninety-five pounds when he was in kindergarten."

Everyone wants to know the star wrestler, shot-putter, and football player, and Rick took to the admiration without losing focus. By high school, he had dedicated himself to football, right offensive tackle, as it became apparent that he had the tools to make it in the pros, or at least get a nice ride to college. He was playing varsity as a freshman, hitting three hundred pounds. But Rick also liked the drinking life. His sophomore year, Hull's grandmother died at the age of fifty-seven. He was very close to her, and it was then that his drinking escalated from hobby to sedative. By his senior year, his partying began to get in the way of football. Or vice versa.

"I played maybe one game sober in my senior year," Hull says. "I had a lousy game. Drunk was normal to me."

Still, there were football scholarships being dangled.

Rick and his mom flew out to Syracuse for a meeting with recruiters. Hull liked the team's aggressive offense and felt he would fit in well.

Rick and his mom also made the drive to Joliet Junior

College in Illinois, where an esteemed football program had graduated several players to the pro ranks.

He was also courted by Indiana University. DuPage made an offer. As the time to commit got closer, Hull was ready to pull the trigger on Syracuse.

Two weeks after his graduation, Rick, celebrating as usual, went to a party in town. He had plenty to drink, and driving home, he was pulled over by the police. The arrest and ensuing driving-while-intoxicated charge sunk his scholarships.

And the loss of the scholarships and the disappointment it caused his mother turned him to drugs, says Meredith Barrows, who was friends with Rick his last two years in high school.

"He had lost his dream," Barrows says. "Before that happened, I never heard of him doing drugs."

"I was so disappointed that I couldn't even think straight," Hull says.

Hull's downward spiral was rapid. He worked for a time as a cashier at a self-serve gas station in Noblesville, where friends and fans could see his lot in life was hardly one of success. "I was well known in the community; I would be at people's home for Thanksgiving; I was a good person," Hull says.

He sank himself.

"I haven't done much in life besides jack off a good football career and knowing to be a great fuck off in Noblesville," Hull would later tell police investigators. He says the same thing now.

On that summer night in July 2000, though, his friends

thought they could cheer up their gentle giant with the acquaintance of a wild woman.

———————

Rick wasn't there for the party that night, but his friends wanted him to meet Sarah, especially after she stripped off all of her clothes and proceeded to make out with another of the girls there, in front of the whole party.

"I called Rick right away and told him that this party was going to keep going the next day and that he had to meet this girl," says Carl Hall, another friend of Hull's. "Rick hadn't ever had a lot of girls anyway, so this was going to be good for him."

"He looked at her and said, 'Wow,'" Harrison says. "They got together that night after the show; no sex, they just talked all night. They were hopped up on drugs, both of them."

Sarah says the meeting was magical; she had gone to the concert with Stephanie Slocum, the day after the first party.

"The house was owned by some guy's parents, and they were always gone and let him have the house for parties," Sarah says. "So we went there first, and Stephanie introduced me to Rick."

"There are not games with this one: he's off the chain," Slocum said as she introduced the two. Hull had a pocket full of ecstasy. He handed Sarah a handful. They got along well.

Sarah would later describe the night in a poem: "One night I went to a Phish concert, blown out of my mind /

I was looking for a good time, what I got was a hot young man who turned my life around."

But for all the fire they struck before, during, and after the show, the two became separated afterward, being so struck by each other they forgot to exchange phone numbers.

Then one afternoon in late July, two weeks later, Sarah, flying on ecstasy with her friend Stephanie in tow, decided that it was time to find this "hot young man" and make him hers. Hull had told her he lived in Noblesville, a nearby exurb. So on this night, Sarah began to drive to Noblesville, where she was convinced she would fetch him.

On the very same day, Rick Hull, tripping on acid after a night working the door at Hoosier Connection Sports Bar, began walking home to Noblesville, a thirty-mile proposition that took him down a major highway. Hull and a friend began the trek as the sun came up, feeding themselves with acid along the way.

"I saw him walking by Ninety-sixth Street, pulled over, and asked him why he hadn't called," Sarah says. The two came together and were rarely seen apart after that. It was a storybook romance, fueled by drugs, alcohol, and those demons that Sarah had fought so hard to exorcise. With Hull, however, she had found a partner who embraced her willful ways.

Sarah soon moved from her one-bedroom apartment, the one she and her mother had fixed up, and within a month, Rick and Sarah were living in a house on Meikel Street just off downtown Indianapolis, taking as roommates a friend of Rick's named Andrew Cataldi and his girlfriend, Tricia Nordman. Both were runaways from the Nevada Department of Corrections, previously locked up on drug charges.

———

Cataldi, known to most as Drew, and Nordman were fugitives from the Nevada Department of Corrections. Drew was troubled from the word go. His father, George, was injured on the job as a New York Police Department officer in the late 1970s, and by 1983, at the age of forty-three, he was deemed too disabled to work. He moved the family—wife Cookie, daughter Karen, sons Steven and Andrew—to a piece of rural Florida land he had purchased in the 1970s. He built a house, and the kids settled into a life of routine that greatly contrasted with growing up in New York City.

"There was nothing, and we really hated it," Andrew's brother Steven says.

Andrew began to roam: Tennessee, Nevada, Indiana, back home, back to Nevada. One day he called his mom from Las Vegas.

"Mom, I saw someone get murdered," Andrew sobbed. "I want to get out of here, I want to come home."

It was Cookie's duty as a mother to protect him. Of course, she let him come home. It lasted barely a month. Andrew refused to get a job.

During his travels to Indiana, Cataldi went to a Grateful Dead concert. It was 1995. Cataldi was once again too high to function, and he lay down on top of a parked van. The cops spotted him and headed over.

"They were going to take him in," Hull says. "But I was working security and told them I would take care of it. And after that, Andrew and I were friends. We kept in touch for the rest of his life."

A few years later, Cataldi was back in Las Vegas, where he had a sordid coterie of street friends. His meth business was flourishing. He called his pal Rick Hull, who was now a full-fledged drug dealer. Maybe he'd like some of this action, Cataldi thought. Sure enough, he was right.

"They thought they were living like the movie *Fear and Loathing in Las Vegas*," says Tabitha Hull, Rick's younger sister, referring to the screen adaptation of Hunter S. Thompson's masterpiece. "They would do nitrous and drive, which isn't safe at all, and they just didn't care."

But the fun ended on a sunny day in August 1999, when police bashed through the door of the cheap motel room the two were staying in, just off the northern end of the Strip. The two had been carousing about the town for several weeks, dealing drugs, cruising with a tank of nitrous oxide in the backseat, taking occasional hits.

Andrew was not paying attention to his own status as a man with a warrant; he wrote his real name on a hotel check-in slip rather than using an alias. Cops routinely check the registry of low-life motels for possible criminals.

Hull and Cataldi were awakened one morning by sheriff's deputies pointing Glocks at their heads.

"Rick called me and told me that the cops kicked in

the door looking for Drew," says Harrison, Hull's high school pal. "I wired him money to come home."

The warrant was for possession of a controlled substance for sale, and Andrew was incarcerated first in a local jail, then in a minimum-security farm on the outskirts of town. Through the winter, on a work-release program, he worked various jobs, generally leaving for the day and returning at night.

By the following summer, though, he had met a fellow inmate named Tricia Nordman, a skinny girl a year his senior who was serving time for writing bad checks in the Reno area. Hull says she was also in the drug game, having burned some Mexican dealers on some meth.

On August 4, 2000, Nordman and Cataldi were part of a low-security corrections team handling hoses, carrying water, and picking up trash for the Nevada Division of Forestry amid an outbreak of wildfires in the foothills of Las Vegas. Andrew had barely three months left on his sentence. But he had been there long enough, he felt, and together that day, he and Tricia walked from the site and headed for the bus station in downtown Las Vegas. They were free, and they were together. Hopping a bus to Florida, Andrew was confident that he would be able to find a hot meal and a place to stay at his parents' home.

From a phone booth, Andrew called them. His dad, fed up with Andrew's antics, which had now reached the level of lawlessness, handed the phone again to Cookie Cataldi.

"Mom, I moved to a halfway house and am trying to

get it together," he told her. Then he lied. "They had us fighting some local fires, wildfires, and told us that when we were done, we could leave. I want to come home, Mom. Please let me come home."

No, Cookie said. She had endured thirteen years of his stories, tall tales, and constant engagements with the law. This time would be no different. No was the final answer.

So Andrew and Tricia headed for the Indianapolis area, where Drew's pal Rick Hull welcomed them at his mom's modest house in nearby Noblesville on August 16. Rick was happy to see his friend, and as for Tricia, well, any friend of Andrew's was fine. The two were tight.

"Drew called Rick his bodyguard," Cookie says. "They were good friends, and Drew had lived [in the Indianapolis area] before. He felt comfortable there."

Since getting locked up the previous year, Andrew had envisioned a drug enterprise, a kingdom in which he was the king. He possessed a chemical-embracing free spirit, and what better way to make his spirit sing than to surround himself with drugs?

In a letter to Hull early in the summer of 2000, Andrew told him of his plan.

"I really do consider you a very close friend of mine and I can trust you," Andrew wrote. "So please stay out of trouble cause I get out in November and I'm sending 4 U . . . and me and you are going into business! Legit!"

He signed the letter, "your homy, Drew."

Once in town, Rick and Drew set up that business,

selling pot, coke, acid. Neither had much inclination to do much inside the law. Both had now done some time in prison, loved the thrill of the drug trade, and knew plenty of outlaws. On August 19, they moved with their respective girlfriends, Sarah and Tricia, into a house in downtown Indianapolis. Andrew handled selling methamphetamine and weed. Rick sold steroids and ecstasy.

Rick had told Sarah about the sordid details of his fun with Andrew up front, and she said she didn't care.

"You ready for a good trip?" Hull asked.

He told her that he and Andrew were going into the drug business together.

"You get the house and we'll pay for it," Andrew said to her.

Again, Sarah said fine.

"Drew and Richard were partners in a drug business that they had established quite some time before I ever met Richard," Sarah said. "The situation was that Drew and Richard were supposed to be equal partners and that I provided a home, a legitimate job and all the cover, quote, unquote, and [Tricia] would just be Drew's girlfriend."

Sarah was proud of her new squeeze, calling her mother one evening and telling her about Rick and her new living arrangement, praising him as any young girl in the blush of fresh love does.

"What does he do?" Bonnie asked her daughter,

pleased that Sarah had met someone who seemed to make her happy.

Sarah hedged a bit.

"He generates income," she said. Her tone was a bit defensive, it seemed to Bonnie.

"What do your roommates do?"

"They also generate income," Sarah said. She was hedging.

"What, do they sell Tupperware door-to-door, what is this?" Bonnie asked. She had been through the experience of having two daughters, Sarah and Jennifer, endure a rough go of living between divorced parents. Drugs, booze, sex, all of it was old hat to Bonnie as a parent, and she quickly realized that the only one gainfully employed in that household was her daughter.

"Sarah, this doesn't sound good, you are the only one working in that house," Bonnie said.

"Mom, I am going to work every day and Rick is good to me," Sarah replied.

It wasn't enough assurance for Bonnie. Two days later, she and her husband, Gene, made the thirty-mile trip to the house on Meikel. When they arrived, Tricia and Andrew were sitting on the couch in the living room, entranced in a video-game version of Monopoly. Only they were not playing it as the deliberate, thoughtful game conceived of by Charles Darrow in 1933. No, this was a live-action, amphetamine-ramped twist on the game as adapted by a couple of tweakers. It was bizarre, and Bonnie had never seen speed freaks in action.

"I had never seen anything move so damn fast in my

life," Bonnie says. "They didn't even turn around and acknowledge we were there."

It was an uncomfortable visit, but Hull was magnanimous and sweet, just as Sarah described him. Bonnie and Gene left. It was unsettling, she said. The neighborhood was lousy; the roommates were sketchy. And even Rick, as nice as he was, was shady.

"But she was twenty-one years old, and I just had to guide her as best I could," Bonnie says. "I said my piece, and Sarah told me, 'I can't help it if you don't like him; I do.' And that's when I realized that I would rather have a relationship with my daughter than to lose it over a choice she made for a mate."

Hull met other family members and left a good impression. One evening shortly after meeting Sarah, the new couple visited Roland's house, a small frame job built in a lake community on an inlet with a boat.

"He was a good-sized guy," recalls Tony Culp, Sarah's uncle. "We talked about how he was thinking about going into professional wrestling, and how he hurt his knee. He was very friendly, very well spoken."

Sarah's aunt Diana saw her around the same time, with Hull in tow.

"It seemed like she wasn't her perky normal self," Diana says. "She was distant. We just didn't see her as much after she met that guy."

———

Tabitha Hull had made friends with Andrew Cataldi during his visits to the Hull home in Noblesville over the previous four years. It was a platonic relationship, and Andrew served as another older brother to her, and like Rick, a drug-addled one at that.

Tabitha liked drugs and drinking, too, like her brother and pal Andrew. She came to the house in Indianapolis to party, to buy pot, and to help sell some pot to folks in Noblesville. But the meth that Andrew was using was changing him. His usual sweet, laid-back disposition was disappearing, replaced by a teeth-grating edge that made her uneasy.

"He would get angry and demanding about even little amounts of money that I would owe him," Tabitha says. "Even $150 and he would get demanding and weird."

One afternoon, Tabitha came to the house and found Rick alone, hanging out, cleaning a bit, listening to music. It was a soft fall day in September, when one begins to notice the yellow shadows draping and the leaves hold the slightest tinge of yellow, and Tabitha recalls how much she really loved her older brother. She was about to turn eighteen and was ready to leave the home she had grown up in, maybe take a roommate. The house on Meikel was giving her some bad vibes. So she took a shot at perhaps getting her brother some peace and herself a roommate she could trust.

"Why don't you and me get a place, just the two of us, and you can get out of here?" she asked Rick that afternoon. "Maybe it's time to get away from all this."

Rick looked at her long. He had Sarah, a woman he loved. No, he said. He couldn't leave now.

———————

A month later, Bonnie and Gene were back down to the house on Meikel for a visit, picking up Sarah to take her out to eat. Again, the experience was unsettling, a trip to a world that the Lifetime network had turned into scary feature flicks for parents of wayward children.

Bonnie went inside to use the bathroom, a last resort because she had hoped that her first time in the house had been her last.

"I went in and Rick was knocking on the door of the roommates," Bonnie said. Andrew and Tricia had the large, front bedroom just off the living room. The phone was in there, and Rick had to make a call.

"Drew came out and started cussing, and Rick's face turned bloodred," Bonnie said.

"There are other people here," Hull hissed at Drew, nodding at Bonnie.

Sarah quickly ushered her mother outside. Once in the car, Bonnie leveled with her.

"Sarah, you can't live like this," Bonnie said.

"Yes, Mom, Rick and I are going to try and get our own place," she said.

"No," Bonnie shot back, not sure her daughter was grasping what she was feeling: her daughter was in danger.

"Seriously, you have to get out of this," Bonnie said. "And I mean very soon."

CHAPTER 4

In the early morning hours of October 24, 2000, a Tuesday, Sarah Pender and her brawny boyfriend, Rick Hull, walked into the Walmart on the south side of Indianapolis.

She was in the throes of love and also smitten with a desire for revenge. Her love was for Hull. The object of her vengeance was Jesse Kutcher, the acquaintance who Sarah claims had raped her earlier in the year, just before Easter, three months before she had met Hull. Hull vowed to "blow the dick off" Kutcher, once she told him, Sarah said. She had been receiving threatening phone messages that she believed were from Kutcher.

"The guy that had raped me had been calling me and harassing me," Sarah said. "I tried to call the police and ask if they could do anything about this. I called the pager companies to see if they could trace him . . . nothing. So [Hull] starts playing on my emotional nerve here because I'm like majorly traumatized by this at this time."

"You know, I can go hurt him," Hull told Sarah.

"OK," Sarah said, thinking Hull would perhaps maim her alleged assailant. She was fine with that; disabling his ability to procreate would be a good thing, she thought. But she said Hull was up for more than just that.

"Rick said, 'I'm going to bomb his house' and I was like 'You can't bomb his house, his parents live there. They didn't do anything,'" Sarah said. "And he was like, 'I'll go in there and I'll pump him up real good and I'll shoot him in his dick.' He was like 'Would that make you happy?' and I was like 'Um' and he was like 'C'mon, I really want to do this for you' and I was like, I'm thinking, you know what, I really wouldn't mind seeing this guy without a penis so he can never rape another woman again, so I'm like 'OK' and he's like 'So, are you going to buy me this gun?' He got me, he got me. So I was like, 'OK.'"

The reason the couple went to that particular Walmart on the bustling U.S. Highway 31 in south Indianapolis, she said, was because the house Kutcher lived in with his parents was in the vicinity.

"I showed Rick where he lived."

With Kutcher in mind, the camouflage Mossberg 12-gauge shotgun Sarah purchased was just right, they concurred.

Hull, six feet five and 300 pounds—"big enough to go bear hunting with a switch" is how a prosecutor later put it—was considered by his friends to be a gentle giant, always eager to please, and when it came to Sarah, "He would do anything for her," says Brian Harrison, Hull's high school friend.

For Hull, five days shy of his twenty-third birthday, it was an incongruous bond, to be sure. Rick was more of a physical giant than a mental one; his prodigious use of psychedelics and pot had turned his already simple mind into something of a cartoon.

In her relationship with Hull, Sarah was running the show, the dominant one. They were always together, it seemed. Hull dropped her at work in the morning and usually picked her up in the evening. Her college career was on hold, but she was quieting down a little bit now that she was in a somewhat bastardized version of domesticity with Hull. She was now earning $13 an hour as a clerk at Carl E. Most & Son, a construction contractor. In addition to his drug dealing, Rick worked low-wage odd jobs, mostly as a bouncer at area nightclubs and watering holes. But his real money came from selling pot, coke, meth, and acid out of the house he and Sarah shared with Andrew Cataldi and Tricia Nordman.

———

The four were living in a perfect neighborhood for an enterprise like drug dealing. The house at 906 Meikel Street was a dusty white clapboard dwelling built in 1918, with a barred security door and a stand-alone mailbox on the small patch of lawn in the front. The house was once a duplex and still had two doors off the front porch, although one was blocked off from the inside. The place offered two bedrooms, a living room, and a bathroom, all well-used and kept in the kind of shape only temporary residents would endure. The walls were painted a version of salmon, the beige carpet was ragged, and the furniture was a mishmash of cast-offs, the centerpiece a cushy blue wraparound sofa.

To the city, the land on which the house was sitting was worth $400, and the house itself, nothing.

Across the street was Babe Denny Park, a city-block-sized playground with a swing set, slide, and basketball court. Most of the homes in the small neighborhood were platted in the 1850s, and they were joined by a Baptist church and a welding supply company, making the entire area a blue-collar urban mix that had once been a safe bet but was then generally just a crime wave unto itself.

To the south of the neighborhood, the elevated Interstate 70 kicked out a round-the-clock sound track of trucks and cars speeding along, complemented by the sound of rubber on the road. To the west, a train yard enriched the urban aural mix with a clanging and steel-on-steel clatter.

From the front of the houses on Meikel, one could enjoy an untarnished view of the Indianapolis skyline, where those who got the right hand dealt to them enjoyed the fruits of the booming city of 800,000 residents. For those on the wrong side of the skyline, like Sarah, Rick, Andrew, and Tricia, well, they carved out their own niche in the black-market economy.

The four paid $750 a month for the run-down house, but it was a typical crash pad for twentysomethings with a taste for the underworld and little motivation to do much other than get high and try to find some fun, and never mind the possible repercussions.

In setting the hierarchy for the household, Andrew and Tricia took the master bedroom and Rick and Sarah the smaller bedroom. Andrew, after all, was the mastermind behind what they hoped would be a profitable drug enterprise.

Sarah was the housemother, the one with the job and the money. She was many things to many people. Even in their little circle of friends and acquaintances, Sarah was the one who had the resources to help. As that circle became peopled with characters of a less-than-stellar virtue, Sarah, with her steady income, could and would help in ways the others couldn't or wouldn't.

She wrote a note to a friend named Corey in mid-August. He was in trouble with the law and needed bail money. Sarah advised him that she would indeed cover his $150 bond and told him that she trusted he would not flee.

But there was a caveat, she added.

"If I pay your bond, and sign it, and you run, you better run until your legs fall off because I will find you and shoot you. Don't think I am playing, either."

It was 7:30 a.m. on Tuesday, October 24, when Sarah and Rick approached the Walmart gun counter. Pam Schifeling came over and asked how she could help.

"I'd like to buy a present for my brother and I'm thinking of a gun," Sarah said. After looking at a number of weapons, Sarah gave the nod to the $350 Mossberg shotgun—some call it a "turkey gun"—as Rick pulled a box of ammo from a display. Sarah filled out the necessary paperwork for an over-the-counter gun sale, a form from the Department of Treasury's Alcohol, Firearms, and Tobacco office. She handed over a check.

She made the purchase in her name because Rick was prohibited from buying a weapon; he had a formidable criminal history, although nothing violent. It was led by two felony convictions, one for auto theft and the other for residential entry. His record was rounded out by misdemeanors, including two convictions for being a minor consuming alcohol and one conviction each for drunk driving, driving with a suspended license, and public intoxication.

Schifeling would later pick Sarah out of a photo lineup as the one who made the purchase.

After dropping Sarah off for work, "Rick went out with a buddy into the country shooting stuff," Sarah said. The country he went to was around his hometown of Noblesville, where he knew the woods and the beautiful back roads.

Many of his friends had remained there, where cornfields and poverty were quickly giving way, even in 2000, to upscale growth that came in the form of strip malls and moneyed commuters seeking the country life.

October 24 was warm and sunny in the countryside, and Hull came back later in the day about the same time Sarah came home from work. Rick was driving a borrowed truck—he had visited his friend Ronnie Herron the night before and borrowed his red 1992 Dodge Dakota. It was a beauty, with an extended cab and $3,000 rims.

Herron lived on two and a half acres in the country northeast of Noblesville, and he and Hull had been pals since "we were real little," Herron said. It was like that with Hull and Noblesville; he had friends everywhere. Hull had even used Herron's truck before, to move. Herron never questioned him about why he needed it. That was what friends were for, he figured.

That particular fall evening, Rick and Sarah were both looking forward to a night out with Sarah's father, Roland, and her stepmom, Sheryl.

"At this point [that day], even though for weeks he had been talking big about shooting someone . . . everything [was] fine," Sarah said. Rick's drug intake, prodigious on a good day, was about average that October day.

"He had done some meth that morning, and maybe some more in the afternoon," Sarah said.

In the evening, Rick and Roland went out for steaks and beer and shot some pool, getting along fine. Sarah and her stepmother went shopping.

The boys got back to Roland's house first, and the two had some small talk until Rick excused himself and went outside to the truck, where he smoked a bowl and took a hit of acid.

Despite a sometimes strained relationship between Sarah and her stepmother, the evening was a success.

Sarah and Rick returned to the house on Meikel around 11 p.m. that Tuesday evening. Sarah, Drew, Tricia, and Rick smoked some of the pot that was always around. Big brown paper bags of it were stashed in a closet, and more was bagged in small quantities for sale.

As the night wore on into early morning, Sarah began to feel sleepy, and while several people came and went to purchase pot, Rick began to argue with Drew over something rather trivial, according to Sarah's account of the evening.

In fact, there are a number of accounts of the evening from around 2 a.m. on, which is about the time things went south on Meikel. Sarah has given a number of different scenarios, and Hull has gone back and forth between claiming to be the triggerman and being gone from the house at the time of the crime.

As statements were compiled and evidence was studied, the most credible account in the eyes of the prosecution was Sarah's, and ironically, it would be that account that would be her undoing. It is that version on which the prosecution relied in its case, and it is the one that most agree is closest to the truth. Hull, though, delivered his account and passed a state-issued polygraph. Some weight needs to be given to that.

Sarah has given two different reasons for an argument that began to unravel the evening of October 24, 2000. The first was over a cell phone and usage that was being racked up by Drew. The other was over a $150 debt for some weed that Rick's sister, Tabitha, owed Drew. Police reports show that Tabitha spoke to Drew at 3 p.m. on the twenty-fourth and made plans to come over to the house the next day to pay up.

Under both of Sarah's accounts, before the argument really grew heated, "I just got up and left. I can't stand to see this stuff," Sarah said. "I didn't have my car, so I couldn't just go for a drive, like I had done before. So I walked out to go get some cigarettes."

She walked three blocks to the east, where a small collection of shops sat on Meridian Street—a main road in Indianapolis that traverses the entire north-south dimensions of the city.

Sarah returned to the house an hour later. It was quiet. She looked in the front window, which looked into the living room. It was dark, with some muted light casting a yellow glare on what appeared to be sleeping people on the floor.

Sarah walked in the front door, and to her right lay the bodies of Drew and Tricia.

"Drew's body is on the floor and Tricia's is on the couch, and [Rick] is standing over them and I thought, 'Son of a bitch, what am I gonna do?'" Sarah said. "I can't run because he'll find me and kill me, so what I need to do is stick around and be loyal. Never in my wildest dream did I think that I was at fault. I knew that this was my gun and my house, but this is what I have to do because I'm his loyal girlfriend and this is what happens in the drug game."

Sarah and Rick began the grim task of moving the bodies, pulling them onto blankets as the blood dripped onto the floor, staining the ragged beige carpet. Working as a team, the couple wrapped their roommates' bodies in blankets and loaded them into the bed of the borrowed truck. It was shortly after 3 a.m. From there, they drove five blocks over to Meridian Street and pulled around the rear of the Edward T. Carlson Hall, home of the local 716 Teamsters. There, the two pulled the wrapped, blood-dripping bodies and tossed them into a small Dumpster, leaving several patches of bright red blood to dry to black on the pavement.

"We went back and rolled up the carpets and shampooed them," Sarah said. "I didn't know how culpable I was, but I said, 'Shouldn't you wipe your fingerprints off?' It seemed like [Rick] had this all figured out."

Sarah punched the clock at 8:09 a.m. on Wednesday, October 25, reporting for work at Carl E. Most & Son, just six hours after witnessing carnage that most people will never have the bad fortune to see. She left for lunch at 12:09 p.m. and returned at 1:11, then left for the day at 5:04 p.m. If the events that went down just a few hours prior had shaken her up, she put forth an acting job worthy of an Oscar.

"I had a meeting in the office that day with an engineer from Chicago, and Sarah was sitting at her desk," says John Most, Sarah's boss. "She had a new outfit and looked really nice, and I told her so."

Although many days Sarah wore jeans and shirts, tidy but nothing fancy, on that Wednesday, she was wearing a businesslike outfit, with black pants and a red blouse. She looked ebullient.

"She was in the best mood I had seen her in for some time," adds Leo DeHerdt, the company's controller.

While Sarah went about her day, Rick toiled at the house, attempting to clean the copious amounts of blood out of the carpet with a rented carpet steamer.

Around 3 p.m., a frequenter of the house, Curtis Willis, called Drew's cell phone and Rick Hull answered. Willis wanted to score.

"They've gone back to Las Vegas, both of them," Rick said. Drew had mentioned to Curtis just the previous night that he was expecting a shipment of methamphetamine to arrive soon. But Rick said no shipment had yet arrived, and he wasn't sure what was going on with it.

"They left all the drugs and their stuff as well," Rick told Curtis. Several hours later, another customer of Drew's, Amanda Miller, called Rick to see what happened to Drew. Same story: "Drew is out of town for a few days. But I have some pot, acid, and coke. Mostly I'm trying to get rid of the weed, if you know anyone."

Tabitha Hull showed up at the house at around 4:30 p.m. to meet Drew as she had previously arranged. What she found startled her: the couch was sitting in the middle of the living room instead of its usual place along one wall. She walked into Drew's be oom, "and it looked like there was some kind of alterca ion . . ." she later told police. Rick told her to leave the room, and she did as her older brother ordered.

She asked where Andrew was. After all, she was there to meet with him, and she was on time.

"He left with some guy," her brother told her.

"Who was the guy?" Tabitha asked.

"I don't know, he didn't come in, I don't know what to do," Rick replied. He didn't seem too concerned, only a bit miffed and slightly ponderous over his friend's abrupt departure. Rick and Tabitha were killing time before picking up Sarah at work, so they chatted while he was puttering about. He brought out his new shotgun to show her.

"Look what I got," he proclaimed brightly.

Tabitha, with no interest in guns, looked away.

The two went to pick up Sarah at work around 5 p.m., and Tabitha immediately noticed something was wrong; "[Sarah] seemed nervous and did not want to go back into the house [on Meikel]," Tabitha said. She left the house around 6 p.m. and headed back for Noblesville, confused and more than a little spooked.

"Something is not right there, something bad happened," she thought to herself.

———

At about the same time Tabitha left, five blocks east, one third of a mile away, Stephen Stultz was wrapping up his day at the Teamsters hall on Meridian Street, where he was director of pensions. Stultz was taking some garbage out to the Dumpster, part of an everyday routine. He lifted the heavy plastic lid off the vessel and tossed the garbage bag in and realized that it had bounced off something. It was dark but Stultz could make out a shape and some color.

"It was the back of a man on the other side of the Dumpster; he had no shirt on, but I really couldn't see much of anything," Stultz says.

It wasn't an uncommon sight in that area to see a bum, looking to sleep it off, finding haven in a garbage bin around the neighborhood. Stultz knew that the city trash pickup was the next morning, and he'd hate to see someone get tossed into the compactor.

"Hey buddy, you OK?" Stultz yelled at the presumably sleeping man while shaking the Dumpster, hoping to roust him up. No response. He walked to the other side of the container and looked in a little closer.

"I looked down inside and saw three legs. I figured it out."

Stultz headed inside to call the police.

When police arrived, they pulled open the container and tried to move the man, who had stiffened. Underneath him, facedown, was another person, a female. Maybe.

"These bodies were atrocious," says Ken Martinez, who led the investigation for the Indianapolis Police Department. "The blood alone was terrible. The bodies were both shot at close range."

Three separate pools of blood, invisible to Stultz in the night darkness, lay coagulating in front of the Dumpster.

Drew was clad in white socks, sandals, and blue jeans. There were $20 packets of methamphetamine in his pant pocket, packaged the way a dealer would know how. Tricia was wearing gray sweatpants, white socks, a sandal on her right foot, and a white Nike T-shirt. Neither had ID. Tricia's face was literally blown off. Tricia's fingerprints could not be taken because of "an oily substance being on her hands," and Andrew's were taken but could not be compared in a database because of "poor quality of the print taken," according to an internal investigation case report.

The bodies were taken to the morgue at Indiana University Medical Center, where doctors found Drew had some unique identifiers: a Grateful Dead tattoo on his left thigh above the name Tricia; a skull engulfed by a spiderweb on his left shoulder; and the number 69, a peace sign, and a Harley-Davidson eagle on his right shoulder.

————

Rick called his friend Brian Harrison on the evening of Wednesday, October 25.

"Bro, I gotta get out of here," Rick said, his voice pitched with anxiety.

"What happened, what's wrong?" Harrison asked.

"I'm into something I don't know that I'll ever get out of," was the ominous reply.

Florida was one of the options Sarah and Rick considered. First, in their panic, they headed for a place they were sure to be found: a small "no-tell motel" called the Mar-Jon Motel, twenty-two miles from the Noblesville home of Rick's mother. The motel was clean but seedy, its green paint chipped and its rooms small and redolent of disinfectant. Many guests stayed on the weekly or monthly plan. The motel was perched between a carpet store and a discount tobacco retail outlet on a main north-south thoroughfare in suburban Anderson, Indiana. Sarah paid in cash when she and Rick checked into room 17 on the evening of Wednesday, October 25, after Rick returned the truck to his pal Ronnie.

They had the shotgun with them. Once they got to their room, the couple slept hard and long. Sarah didn't make it to work the next day.

At 11 a.m. Thursday, October 26, pictures of the tattoos were broadcast on local television. By 1 p.m., police had a call from Jana Frederick, a neighbor and customer at the house on Meikel. The bodies were those of Andrew and Tricia, the cops were told. And others were seeing the tattoos on TV and having some bad feelings.

"The news kept talking about these bodies being found and how no one could find out who they were," says Meredith Barrows, a friend of Hull's who dated Drew in 1997. "I was watching that; then they showed Drew's tattoos, and my stomach hit the floor."

Several others also identified Drew by the tattoos. It was a short step to identifying Tricia. And an even shorter step to the house on Meikel, where police arrived at 1:20 p.m. on Thursday. Within thirty minutes, the landlord was on the premises, handing over the names of Sarah Pender and Rick Hull.

———

Later that day, Rick and Sarah went down to the house on Clinton Street. Tabitha was home from high school, where she was a senior. Her mother had left to visit relatives in Tennessee earlier in the day, and Tabitha took the day off to finish some schoolwork on her own.

"When Rick got here, the first thing he did was give me a big hug," Tabitha says. "And there was a look he had that told me things were not right. Drew was dead, and I began to think they had something to do with it. And before that, it was unthinkable."

The three of them took off in an effort to sell a half pound of pot Rick had. The money it would fetch could stake them to some time on the run.

———

At the house on Meikel, Detective Ken Martinez was in the middle of another fifteen-hour day. A guy who could go for days with little sleep, Martinez was invaluable to Lieutenant Mark Rice at the Indianapolis Police Department. He was a primary cog in a department that proudly boasted a solve rate of around 70 percent, as compared to the national average of 62 percent. The city had around 130 murders a year in the early 2000s. It was enough to keep everyone busy all the time.

"Kenny was balls to the wall," Rice says. "His style was not polished, but he would go until he dropped. His motivation was high, and he took cases personally."

Ken Martinez was thirty-six years old with nine years with the Indianapolis PD, had already been through two short-lived marriages, and was no stranger to late-night carousing and enthusiastic drinking, which most blamed for the quick dissolution of his marriages. Martinez was a beefy, well-developed man whose barrel chest curved into the coveted V-shaped body that many men work years to develop. His black hair was barely an inch long all around, and his height, six feet, presented an impressive physical presence. Martinez also had a unique identifier: a stutter that at times threatened to turn a five-minute verbal exchange into a quarter-hour episode. But there was one time that stutter would disappear: "When Kenny was smooth-talking the ladies, there was no stutter, not even a hitch," Rice says.

Tips began to fly in as soon as word of the murders hit the neighborhood. The postman, the guy in the house on the other side of the street, more drug customers—they all rolled info. Drew was well liked, not just by his customers but by people in the neighborhood. His customers were outraged and were more than willing to help, even if it meant handing out information on Sarah and Rick, who were also regarded as decent, if misguided.

By 3 p.m. Thursday, a search warrant was signed, and crime technicians were inside the house on Meikel. Hull's identification was found, showing a home address at his mother's, 1084 Clinton Street, in Noblesville.

Rice and another detective, Anthony Finnell, drove up to the corner-lot house and were joined by a handful of officers and detectives from the Noblesville Police Department. The team set up around the Clinton Street address, manning the periphery, and Finnell knocked on the door. No answer. He got back into the unmarked Crown Victoria with Rice. It was now dark out, and anyone coming into or out of the house would not likely be able to see that the place was surrounded. The cops could wait. But they didn't have to.

"Just like that, a car pulls up with Rick driving, Sarah and Tabitha as passengers," Rice says. "They got out of the car in the driveway, and we were on them fast, shotguns, handguns all pointed at them. Tabitha was screaming; this really rocked her world in a bad way. She knew what was going on, and she was scared out of her mind."

The car was Sarah's aged silver Cavalier. The trio was taken the three blocks to Noblesville police headquarters, and the scrutiny began. It was 11 p.m. Thursday night. The cops had already solved the case after barely forty-eight hours.

―――――――

"Sarah was ready to roll on Hull right away," Martinez says. "She was very intelligent—you knew that right away. And she was very sexual. She's not a great beauty. She was heavyset, big boned, but she comes off very sensual in her body movements. She didn't have the looks, but she sure had the personality. She tried to mentally seduce you. I told her that we needed to talk about what happened, and she was batting her eyelashes at me and being very nice. I closed it down. I wasn't about to play that shit."

The officers were focusing on Hull as the primary suspect. Few females kill in such a direct and violent fashion. And from the outset, Sarah cooperated.

She turned over a pair of Hull's black pants, which had blood on them that was later found to be that of Drew and Tricia. She told them that she had seen Rick stash some blood-soaked cushions from a love seat at the house on Meikel into a plastic bag. There was too much blood, she said.

"I freaked out, and seeing little bits and pieces of people strung across my house is not really the best thing for my soul to see," she told Martinez. "I've never seen a dead carcass look like that, and it was really gross."

But after two hours, she stopped. She was tired. She was smart enough to know how to end the questioning; she asked for a lawyer. It was 1 a.m. on October 27. For her trouble, she was an overnight guest at the Noblesville jail.

———

Rick Hull was even more voluble than Sarah. He talked for hours and told Martinez and Rice that the whole thing came down in a much different fashion than Sarah was telling. Drew and Tricia left with an unknown party on Tuesday night, according to Hull. The bodies were found; he and Sarah saw the television broadcast and moved to a motel, fearing some deranged drug-dealer killer. The motel rate was $27.50 a night, Hull added.

"That's not bad," Martinez remarked.

"No, that ain't bad at all," Rice chimed in. "So which broadcast did you happen to watch?"

More talk, making it friendly. Hull kept with the story. Drew was violent on occasion, verbally abused Tricia. The four all liked going to bars, to "have a few drinks."

Drew left his cell phone at the house when he left with the mysterious party, Hull said.

Fifteen minutes into the interview, Rice read Hull his rights.

"Does that mean I'm under arrest when the rights are read to me?" Hull asked.

"No, no, no, huh uh," Martinez assured him.

Within thirty minutes, Hull's world came apart at the hands of Martinez, who was no longer his friend.

The detective hit Hull with the blood in the house, statements from witnesses, "blood on the ceiling," and the very clothes the two victims died in.

"What were you thinking when this went down?" Rice asked him.

Hull sputtered. His kid sister, Tabitha, owed Drew money, he said. Then he let it go.

"And he and I got into an argument that night, he knew that I had the [shotgun], he went in my room to try to grab it, got in a little struggle, he said he was going to kill my fucking family. . . . So right now, I'd not like to answer any more questions 'cause I have a feeling I'm going to be arrested."

Martinez, now clearly enraged, bellowed, "Now I'm not going to question you any more but just keep in mind one thing: You have got to explain three shots, a 290-pound man that outweighs two people by quite a bit, this is your only chance to explain this, if you want that, that's fine.

"But you are under arrest for murder times two."

It was 6 a.m. on October 27, a dark and cold morning. The house Rick Hull grew up in, where he lived a football star's high school life, was just eight short blocks away, a two-minute walk. And his freedom was removed forever.

———

Police searched Sarah's car and found little. They took two cell phones, some clothing, and a Tupperware container filled with marijuana. Thinking Sarah would be a key witness and not wanting to discourage her with a minor possession charge, Martinez simply turned it over to the property room. It would later be determined that the weed belonged to Tricia and that the container was what she always used to carry her stash in. It was one more link in a delicate chain connecting Sarah inextricably to the murder.

———

The night in jail was unpleasant enough for Sarah. While Hull was being arrested, she was ready to help the cops

some more. This time, she was going to take them to the
Mar-Jon Motel and help them get the murder weapon.
Ken Martinez showed up with a crime technician and a
search consent form for the motel room.

They almost didn't make it.

"I hadn't slept at all the night before because we were
working, trying to put together search warrants, and the
call from Noblesville came pretty early; it was like 7:45
a.m.," Martinez says. "So I put Pender in the back of the
car with the guy from the crime lab and start driving the
twenty miles or so to the motel. It's a two-lane road that
I took, and I fell asleep on the way and crossed the cen-
terline. I woke up to Sarah and the crime lab guy yelling
at me to wake up."

The weapon was recovered in room 17 and sent to the
lab for analysis. Having nothing more to hold Sarah for,
she was released to her father, Roland.

By 2 p.m. on Friday, October 27, Martinez was running on fumes, and Rice told him to go home. His ace
detective had wrung up twenty-nine hours of overtime in
two days and had almost killed a key witness.

———————

The next day, Saturday, October 28, at 9 a.m., Martinez
visited the Walmart where the weapon was purchased.
He had found the receipt for the gun at the motel. Just to
make sure, he wanted to see who had paid for it. He
knew that Hull had a criminal record and would never
have passed even the brief background check retail gun
sellers must run.

Martinez was a little startled when he saw Sarah had both signed for and paid for the gun. The clerk told him it was odd to have someone buy that particular Mossberg model, often preferred by turkey hunters because of its long barrel and pump action, and deer slugs, which are larger and better for bringing down larger prey. Martinez agreed. Unless the intent was to murder someone, perhaps.

With the evidence of the weapon purchase, Sarah was now an accessory to murder. Getting her to the Indiana Police Department headquarters was easy; Martinez called Roland Pender and said he had some clothes from the house on Meikel that he believed were hers. Could he bring Sarah down to retrieve them?

They arrived at 11 a.m., and Martinez asked if she would talk a little more. She agreed. He confronted her about the weapon purchase, which she admitted. Sarah was arrested quickly.

Roland was immediately angry.

"You hoodwinked me," he said to Martinez and Finnell, who jointly made the arrest.

"Your other choice was having a SWAT team knock in your door," Finnell said. "Isn't this easier and less traumatic?"

Sarah stood cold, Martinez said.

"She never broke down even a little," he says. "She went from being a warm sexual being to a cold bitch, even when she was confronted with the evidence."

"I didn't do it and I'll be out of here," Sarah told Martinez. And she asked again for a lawyer. It was something she would sorely need.

CHAPTER 5

It took two years to get Sarah's case to the courtroom, a case mired in motions and maneuvers.

Hull had not yet gone to trial, his case being delayed until 2003 by a series of motions and smart lawyering that aimed to put as much time as possible between the crime and the trial.

Behind the scenes, in advance of her trial, the drama played out largely because of Sarah's behavior. Her prolific letter writing ended any chance she had at getting out of a lengthy prison sentence.

She attempted to seduce any male within writing distance with her wordy letters written with flowery prose in ornamental handwriting. She promised sex, freedom, and blessings in her missives to other inmates and to her partner, Richard Hull, who responded in kind, only with feeling. The promises no doubt influenced his statements to the police. Yes, he killed them. No, Sarah killed them, back and forth Hull went. Hull was clueless as to what to do, confused by letters pledging hate, then love, from Sarah.

Letters between locked-up codefendants are prohibited, but she managed to find a go-between on the outside, Dawn Roedale, a mutual friend, to launder the letters, which she sent on to Hull.

"Yep, it's been a year," Sarah wrote in a July 15, 2001, letter, noting the anniversary of their meeting at the Phish concert. "In a way, it's been agonizing as all Hell, but in retrospect, it's not as bad as it could be."

She allowed that she loved him and that she was thankful to have experienced his "tender heart and sweet side."

Another letter from Sarah changed the tenor of their missives abruptly, with a double shot of disdain for Hull: "Do you think your sin will go unpunished?" Sarah asked. "Do you think trying to condemn an innocent person to a life sentence will never come back to haunt you?"

Still another encouraged Hull to hand himself in and pledged her fealty to him while he was incarcerated. She vowed to stay with him, even if he was locked up and she was free. She would work on their life.

"I'm not leaving you just because you may get time. I won't leave you, even if you get a really long time in prison."

Her idea of an ideal life, cliché as it was, came through as she asked Hull, "Why can't we be living comfortably

in our ranch or farm home in the country, with the 2½ car
garage and the dog in the yard?"

She wanted kids, marriage, the American Dream.
From her perspective, sitting in a jail cell, any twist on
freedom seemed appealing. She would get out and go
straight, she said in her letters. No more boozing ways,
no carousing, no drugs. No street life. And her letters to
Rick vowed to make him part of the whole change.

Sarah's affections were generous, of course; even in
the Marion County Jail, she gained a reputation as a
manipulative con artist who was brazen in her efforts
to get something from everyone. One of her cons fell
on a lifetime criminal named Floyd Pennington, a slow-
witted sex offender who also had raps for robbery, theft,
and battery. He was awaiting trial on a robbery charge
and had been in the jail for ten months while his case
was sorted out. Over the summer, Sarah and Pennington
exchanged nearly eight letters while, at the same time,
Sarah was writing with promises of sexual favors and
lifetime commitment to Hull.

Sarah and Pennington met at a Catholic mass service
a few weeks after she was arrested. Sarah would take
five days penning him sixteen-page heartfelt notes beaming with almost pathological exuberance.

"I think what we share is way too special to risk con-
taminating it with overactive sexual content," she wrote
in a letter dated June 14, 2001.

Another letter in September oozes of her excitement
at seeing him during a prisoner transfer, when inmates

are gathered for transport to the courthouse for their respective appearances: "I . . . loved being able to look at you [and] soak in your body, your face, the way your face moves when you say 'I love you!'"

But her clumsy jailhouse wardrobe was hardly what he deserved, she said.

"Do you really know how hard it is to be cute and sexy in a set of belly chains and leg shackles? Of course you do. But I do not ever worry about being anything other than me, just me, all me."

The sometimes-bizarre exchanges also included snipes at the intelligence of the prosecutor's office and the likelihood that the charges against her could be beat. Sarah thought she was smart enough to outwit a system that had been locking people away for generations, and she almost said as much. This, despite the fact that the prosecutor's office at that point was not intent on pursuing the same hefty murder conviction it was seeking for Hull. Evidence showed that, indeed, Sarah was a bright girl who had a severe lapse of reason. Instead, she could plead to something else. A low-level felony, which would have netted her two to eight years in prison, was being considered in exchange for her testimony against Hull.

———

All of Sarah's letters out of the jail were being monitored by the prosecutor's office and became fodder for daily dissection as well as being possible evidence.

"I would put these quotes on my door so people knew what was going on," says Kathy Cronley, who worked the case as a paralegal for the Marion County prosecutor's office. Among her duties was compiling these letters, which soon became evidence of Sarah's almost compelling need to manipulate anyone who might be able to help her.

"It was almost like comedy, these letters that Sarah wrote to everyone," Cronley says. "She would be professing her love for Richard Hull, then Floyd Pennington."

"I am not going to run out and find a replacement for you," Sarah pledged in one letter to Hull. "How could I? It would be impossible. I don't think about other men or desire the company of anyone other than you."

A week later, she called Hull an "asshole" after learning that he had been discussing his own version of the murder.

"A snitch and his statement," Sarah accused, pinning Hull with a prison moniker that can spell death. A snitch is the lowest form of prison life. She told Hull that she had received information that he was implicating her in the shooting, although she conceded she didn't know exactly what he was telling the cops.

"You know I didn't have a thing to do with this. I am sitting here because I kept my mouth shut," she wrote.

The letters were unfiltered, and the prosecutors began to see that offering Sarah that deal wasn't such a good idea. She was as culpable as Hull.

Then there was the scratch-and-sniff letter.

Cronley and Ken Martinez, the Indianapolis Police Department detective who had made the case, were in Cronley's office going over the letters. Because they were the original letters, Cronley donned some rubber gloves to handle them. Martinez declined her generous offer to share. Until a few minutes later, when he was reading one of the letters.

"He screamed like a girl and threw the letter he was reading up in the air," Cronley says. "It contained a scratch-and-sniff specially made by Sarah," in which Sarah claimed to have smeared some of her body fluids on the paper.

Martinez grabbed some gloves.

From her cell in the Marion County Jail, Sarah spoke with certainty in letters to friends and family that she would be out among the free in no time, letting one pal know that she needed a "long vacation from this Hell . . . but the only vacation I'm gonna get is my release."

———————

In the early summer of 2001, Sarah's father, Roland, went to an esteemed local attorney, Robert Hammerle. Bearded, erudite, and deeply absorbed by cinema, Hammerle was a high-priced player, to be sure. He was a big fish in Indiana's biggest pond of Marion County, and he knew his way around the criminal element. But his first visit to Sarah in the Marion County Jail showed him a young woman who clearly stood out among her criminal colleagues.

"There are times when you visit people in jail and the first thing you think to ask is, 'What the hell are you doing here?'" Hammerle says. "It's almost like someone won a bad lottery ticket. I genuinely liked her. This was a young woman who could [make] some contributions and be loved as someone's next-door neighbor, and no one would ever have known about this."

The fact that a Class C felony was on the table, after some negotiation by Hammerle, was almost a legal miracle. It looked to everyone like Hull was the prime mover in the murders, and Sarah's only crime was being in love with him.

The deal was proceeding with some resistance from the prosecutor's office. They now felt that the case against both Sarah and Rick was strong, and Sarah would come back from her visits with Hammerle discouraged. Sometimes, when her parents would visit—her father, Roland, on Wednesdays; her mother, Bonnie, on Thursdays—she would return to her cell in tears. Neither parent was feeling good about the deal for immunity.

"Her mom said, 'No, they wouldn't offer immunity,'" said Lisa Massimino, who shared a cell with Sarah, sleeping in the upper bunk.

"My mom doesn't seem like she's very hopeful that I'm going to get out of this," Sarah told her after one visit from her mother.

"That's when she came back all crying and upset," Massimino said. "She had even made a statement to me that as much as she loved [Hull], to save her own ass, she would, if they were going to offer her immunity or something, testify against him, that he had more or less done this, if it would get her out of this."

Still, the deal for the lower felony was on the table. If she could just hold on and act right.

Then one day in late July, shortly before the deal was to be consummated, Hammerle was summoned to the prosecutor's office and presented with a batch of letters written by Sarah to Hull. In a search warrant served July 17, 2001, at the Marion County Jail, prosecutors took fifty-one pieces of correspondence from Hull's cell and five from Sarah's. Most of them were from Sarah to Hull. In them, the prosecutors showed Hammerle what ranks among a defense lawyer's worst fears.

In the letters, Sarah asserted to Hull that they would both be able to walk even though they had killed two people, that the victims deserved it, that the cops and prosecutors were "too stupid" to nail them, and, as an encore, noted that Hammerle was also stupid. The lawyer read the letters and promptly withdrew from the case.

"In effect, the letters to [Hull] not only incriminated herself, but she was taking the position that if they both say nothing . . . that they would both end up walking free," Hammerle says. "Her letters contradicted the idea that she was peripherally involved, as we had been making a case for with the prosecutor's office. Although they could have convicted her, they clearly wanted testimony against the one responsible for it. There was even a sinister quality to these letters from her."

There would be no deal, he knew. These letters would send her down. He went to the jail to tell Sarah before breaking the news to her parents. Neither task would be easy, but at least Sarah would realize what she had done. Her parents had no idea how this could fall apart. She was mere days away from a sentence that could have had her on the street in two years. With time served, Sarah could have been celebrating Christmas in 2003 as a free woman.

But that was not going to happen.

"My God, young lady, look in the mirror," he said to her. "You alone have brought on a prison sentence that may keep you in here, at best, until you are an old woman. I don't understand, but I am withdrawing."

With that, he walked out and never saw her again. Sarah's father was devastated.

"She has literally snatched defeat from the jaws of victory," Hammerle told Roland Pender. "She has left me in an untenable position. The dam has burst, and it is going to roll over her and all because of what she has done with these letters."

Sarah's case was handed over to the public defender's office, never a good turn. Her future fell to James Nave, a former prosecutor turned court-appointed defense lawyer who had very little enthusiasm for the case.

Now the prosecutor's office moved full speed ahead to put both Sarah and Rick away for a long time. They'd show Sarah who was stupid.

———

On September 19, 2001, Floyd Pennington contacted Detective Ken Martinez, the lead investigator in the case. He told Martinez about the letters and that he and Sarah had been corresponding for nine months and that he wished to turn state's evidence on Pender.

"I can get her to tell me things," Pennington told

Martinez. He admitted he was looking for a break on a motion for modification of his potential sentence. Floyd's case was a wisp of air compared to the murder trial. It was a possibility, though no promises were made.

Pennington had already set in motion a plan, with the assistance of the state, to meet Sarah at Wishard Memorial Hospital so the couple could talk without the hindrance of guards or screened letters. On September 22, both complained simultaneously of illness; Pennington's affliction was kidney pain. They were each taken to the hospital's emergency ward, and the plan worked.

For three hours, Sarah and Pennington conversed, lying just twenty-five feet apart. At one point, they were virtually next to each other, Pennington claimed.

A week later, Pennington met with Martinez and told him of his meeting with Sarah.

"She basically told me that the money and the dope, the drugs had been ripped off from them, she was extremely outraged about that, so what she did was use Rick, you know, as a pawn to commit those murders. She basically was the brains and he was the, you know, muscle," Pennington told the detective.

"She had went and purchased the shotgun, you know, that the murders were committed with and then I basically asked her, you know, what, how could she go about doing that and she said that it was out of outrage, you know. All her life she's been going through a lot of things and she said it all just came out and she put Rick up to doing the murders."

There was little doubt that Pennington needed some help from the system himself, but the prosecution decided that he was still credible in that he had actually talked to Sarah.

Pennington later testified in court that Sarah told him she "pretty much" coerced Hull to pull the trigger, that she "had no feelings for the victims and showed no emotion or remorse, she planned to have Hull commit the murders, she was in another room in the house when Hull committed the murders and she would continue to control and manipulate Hull."

Pennington was sentenced eleven days after his court testimony to twelve years in prison in a plea agreement.

But still, there was a problem with his testimony and, in the rearview mirror, its impact on the jury. A letter discovered after the trial in the police file found that Pennington had offered to turn evidence on a list of people, from drug dealers to chop-shop owners. He named names on a yellow legal pad in his own writing. But the list was never presented by the defense during Sarah's trial.

"I never saw that list, and it would seem that the defense never saw it either, since it wasn't in evidence or used to combat Floyd's statements for us," says Larry Sells, who prosecuted the case for the state.

———

Deputy prosecutor Larry Sells wanted to be a lawyer from the time he was in high school in Williamsport, Indiana. The town of barely one thousand people sat between Indianapolis and Bloomington on the Wabash River, and Sells was the son of a World War II air gunner and a secretary.

Sells spent time as a defense lawyer shortly after graduating law school in 1972.

"When I got out of law school, I thought I was going to be rich and famous, which is why I went into defense work," Sells says. "But I didn't get rich or famous."

Instead, he joined the Marion County prosecutor's office, spending 1978 to 1980 putting the bad guys away. Politics drove him out, and he was still looking to get himself a little fame. So as he worked for an Indianapolis law firm, he began to do some modeling, using his Marlboro Man looks to his advantage. There were TV commercials and some print work and one campaign for Southern Comfort that went national, and the work got him some local attention. Then one day, he decided to take a trip to Los Angeles, get an agent, and see if he could find his fame as a model or actor. He was forty years old, though, which worked against him despite his youthful appearance. Without a Hollywood history, Sells would never be the next John Wayne.

Tall and broad-shouldered, Sells's wide, masculine face was framed by a sheath of feathered chestnut hair and a mustache that conjured images of Tom Selleck, the iconic 1970s private detective known as Magnum P.I.

"I was there for six months, and I realized it just wasn't going to happen for me," Sells says. He had his job as a lawyer back home and returned, not with his tail between his legs, but something close to that.

It turned out that the courtroom presented his platform for whatever fame he might achieve, given his bent for theatrics and the law.

A formidable swagger and a tendency to crease his brow to emphasize the seriousness of whatever situation he might be engaged in made the now fifty-six-year-old Sells a tough customer who prevailed with an alarming success rate. He entered the courtroom with a string of fifty-some consecutive felony convictions. In 1997, Sells tried and won fourteen murder cases. He was a tough guy.

Enter Sarah, alleged violent killer who had managed to talk her way out of trouble her entire life. Sells was already itching for a shot at her after the discovery of the letters casting his crew as fools.

On Monday, July 22, 2002, in his opening statement to the jury, Sells allowed that Sarah may not have actually pulled the trigger that killed two people. But she was the one who urged her companion, Richard Hull, to commit the murders.

"Sarah Pender decided she didn't want these folks in there anymore," Sells told the jury in a baritone edgy with anger. "At the very least, Ms. Pender manipulated Richard Hull into committing these murders and she was with him every step of the way."

Among the empanelled jury were a housewife, a secretary, a teacher, an engineer, an auto appraiser, and a registered nurse: eight women, four men.

The defense didn't have a chance against Sells's penchant for drama. At one point in the trial, Sells took the role of Andrew Cataldi, kneeling on the floor of the courtroom while paralegal Cronley held the murder weapon to his chest and played out the murder.

The bombastic playacting was a brutally literal example of Sells's prosecution style: flash, drama, and heavy on the portrayal of brutality. Most prosecutors couldn't get away with such a thing, and some would even face sanction. But Sells was a highly regarded official, and his work often had flourishes such as this.

Also introduced was a letter produced by Richard Hull, allegedly written by Sarah and mailed to him in the fall of 2001.

"I wish I could go back and change the events of that night," the letter said. "Drew was so mean that night. I just snapped. I didn't mean to kill them. It must have been the acid. When you said that you would try and take the blame, I knew then that you loved me deeply. At first, I thought you [would] tell but you stuck to your promise. As time goes on I hope and pray that you beat this."

The letter was analyzed for the prosecution by a state forensics handwriting analyst, Lee Ann Harmless, who concluded that Sarah was the author of the letter. An examination of the letter also found fingerprints belonging to Steve Logan, an inmate who shared a cell in the county jail with Hull.

The defense never produced its own analysis of the letter. Sarah maintained the letter was written by someone else. Hull's sister, Tabitha, came in and gave a handwriting sample. Not her. The letter was a crucial part of the evidence against Sarah.

At one point during the three days of testimony, the

jury had cleared the courtroom and spectators were filing
out when Sarah and Sells found themselves a few feet
apart, fairly alone amid the lowering buzz. She sat, waiting for the bailiff to take her to a holding cell during a
lunch break. Sells was pulling together some papers.

"I hope you can realize that I did not do this," Sarah
said, looking sideways at Sells as she remained seated.
Sells, a gentleman who could not find it in his makeup to
be rude, looked back. The smile that met his gaze was
demure, creased with a slightly seductive pursing of the
lips. It was not unpleasant to look at. This was Sarah's
stock-in-trade, a look that had gotten her what she wanted
for so long. It transcended her bouts with obesity, her
sometimes nefarious intentions, and her self-absorbed
nature.

"Sarah, if you can find something that tells me that
you were not involved in this, just do so," Sells said.

Sarah looked away as she was removed to her lunch,
leg chains clinking in the now-empty courtroom.

During key emotional testimony in the trial, Sarah
would tear up when appropriate, such as when Detective
Ken Martinez spoke of the condition of the bodies. And
when the testimony was completed, Sarah was back to
smiling and conversing with her defense team.

As for Sarah's character, Sells didn't need to dirty her
up. He had already referred to her during proceedings as
"the female Charles Manson," and in his closing, on July
24, at a time when the 9/11 attacks were still fresh in the
minds of Americans, Sells lifted his voice a few decibels.

"Sarah Pender may not be an Osama bin Laden, who

killed thousands of people, but she's a domestic terrorist nonetheless."

He had put forth three scenarios that all spelled a long time in prison for Sarah: that she pulled the trigger, that Rick pulled the trigger and she helped clean up the mess, or that Rick pulled the trigger with her encouragement.

Defense attorney Nave argued that the incriminating letter, which he said was forged by Hull, "was written for another audience. 'I didn't mean to kill them. It must have been the acid.' That says, 'Hey prosecutor, wake up, make a deal.'"

Hull was the shooter of his own volition, Nave said.

"The prosecution would have you believe that Sarah was a clever criminal mastermind and that she's the shooter," he said. "This was not a cleverly planned criminal act. It was an act of the moment."

It didn't wash with the jury. Sells couldn't lose. Sarah couldn't win.

The jury came back within twenty-four hours: guilty on two counts of murder. Sentencing was scheduled for August 22.

———

Marion Superior Court judge Jane Magnus-Stinson was a hard-line judge who would not accept death-penalty cases. She just didn't believe in that kind of justice. Any other lawfully administered punishment, though, was fair game.

Onetime legal counsel to Indiana governor Evan

Sarah Pender, right, at age three, with older sister, Jennifer, in the kitchen of the Pender home in Greencastle, Indiana. —*Courtesy Bonnie Prosser*

Sarah, age seven, at a fair in Santa Claus, Indiana.

—*Courtesy Bonnie Prosser*

Sarah, age ten, fourth-grade class picture.
—*Courtesy Bonnie Prosser*

Sarah, age fourteen, in the summer of 1993, at a park near the family's
Indianapolis home.   —*Courtesy Bonnie Prosser*

Sarah, age eighteen, with her father, Roland, after her high school graduation ceremony.
—*Courtesy Bonnie Prosser*

Richard Hull was a high school football star, playing offensive tackle at Noblesville High School outside of Indianapolis. This was taken his senior year.
—*Courtesy Tabitha Hull*

Andrew Cataldi, right, was Richard Hull's best friend. This photo was taken in 1994. Andrew poses with his older brother, Steven, left, and mother, Cookie, center. —*Courtesy of the Cataldi family*

House at 906 Meikel Street in Indianapolis, where Sarah, Richard Hull, Andrew Cataldi, and Tricia Nordman lived starting in August 2000. In October, Hull and Pender killed Cataldi and Nordman inside the home. —*Indianapolis Police Department*

Detective Ken Martinez of the Indianapolis Police Department could work a case for days with no sleep. He worked the double homicide that sent Sarah to prison for one-hundred-and-ten years.

— Indianapolis Police Department

LEFT:
Captain Mark Rice, now head of homicide for the Indianapolis Metropolitan Police Department, oversaw the police investigation of the murders of Andrew Cataldi and Tricia Nordman.   *—Indianapolis Police Department*

RIGHT:
Larry Sells, deputy prosecutor in Marion County, called Sarah Pender "the female Charles Manson" for her ability to manipulate people into carrying out her murderous intentions.   *—Courtesy Larry Sells*

Sarah Pender, U.S. Marshals Service Most Wanted, the first woman to hit the list in years.

—Courtesy of the U.S. Marshals Service

Sarah smiles as she sits in the backseat of a U.S. Marshals car for the drive back to the Indiana prison system on December 23, 2008. She was captured the night before.
—*Courtesy of* America's Most Wanted

Ryan Harmon, right, the Indiana State Police investigator who worked tirelessly to capture Sarah as part of the U.S. Marshals Service task force, escorts Sarah into the prison in Indiana. Willard Plank, left, director of internal affairs for the Indiana Department of Correction, assists.

—*Courtesy of* America's Most Wanted

Sarah casts her last glance before re-entering the Indiana prison system after spending one-hundred-and-thirty-six days on the lam.
—*Courtesy of* America's Most Wanted

A tearful Sarah Pender tells *America's Most Wanted*, "I'm not proud of some of the things I had to do in order to get out of prison."

—*Courtesy of* America's Most Wanted

Sarah, in her cap and gown, graduated in spring 2008 with her associate's degree while in Rockville Correctional Facility. —*Courtesy Bonnie Prosser*

Bayh, the judge was a strong believer in making the sentence fit the crime. Hailing from Wisconsin, Stinson graduated from Butler University and Indiana University School of Law before heading into her high-ranking job for the governor. And it was all uphill from there. While working for Bayh, she met William Stinson—at the governor's inauguration, in fact—and later married him, and William went on to become executive director of the Indiana State Fair Commission, making the pair into a fairly powerhouse professional couple. Magnus-Stinson was appointed to the bench in 1995 and had presided over dozens of murder trials. William was busy reviving the state fair, which reached record attendance the summer of Sarah's trial.

In the days preceding the sentencing, Magnus-Stinson received letters from Sarah's family and friends, beseeching the judge to consider leniency in her case. One of Sarah's uncles, Tony Culp, claimed that "Sarah was somewhat naive about the man that got her involved in this whole ordeal." Another family friend, Luz Isabel Gonzalez, introduced herself as a pen pal of Sarah's whose mother was friends with Sarah's mom.

Sarah "gives good advice and has a highly moral perspective," Gonzalez told the judge. "I believe Sarah would be a great asset to her community."

And Taylor Walters, who went to high school with Sarah and visited her at the Marion County Jail, vowed to help Sarah if she were to be freed.

"A sentencing that is designed to bolster the support

mechanisms Sarah is trying to create would be ideal,"
Walters said, adding that she hoped for " . . . restorative,
not retributive, justice to this tragic situation."

Sarah's mother, Bonnie, was more realistic, noting
that she made no excuses for her daughter's involvement in the crime, but Sarah "was taken in with this
Rick, that he told her what she wanted so desperately to
hear, that he loved her and would take care of her and all
the rest of the lines men use to get what they want. What
she did is not in her character and she was into a lot of
drugs at the time of this awful crime."

Bonnie enclosed a sheaf of academic plaudits and
certificates of accomplishments that Sarah had earned as
a young girl.

Then there were those who blamed the murder fully
on Hull. One petitioner, Sharon Stockberger, asserted
that Sarah was a "victim of an evil dominate."

The families of the victims also weighed in; one letter
went to the district attorney's office and was entered into
the case file.

"I cannot imagine what was in my brother's mind
when he was being brutally shot by Sarah Pender and
Richard Hull," wrote Karen Dixon, Andrew Cataldi's sister, in a letter also signed by her parents, who had been
married for fifty-eight years when Andrew was killed. "It
sends chills up my spine to think that these two murderers are still breathing. I could only wish for life without
parole."

The presentence report for Sarah portrayed an unlikely murderer. Few priors, save for the theft of her

mother's car and a forgery rap that got her probation. She worked at Carl E. Most & Son from August 1998 to October 1999, then for insurance giant accounting firm Crowe doing books from October 1999 to May 2000, when she returned to Most.

The report noted her being treated for ten days at age fifteen on an inpatient basis at a local community home for depression before moving on to group therapy at seventeen. Her history of drug use showed little out of the ordinary: "Social drinker at 15–16, started pot, her use of the drug increased after she left Purdue University to almost daily . . . also has used [ecstasy] and coke."

The judge had some room in handing down a sentence, but no matter what, Sarah was going away for a while. Magnus-Stinson could give Sarah as low as forty-five years for each murder or up to sixty-five years for each murder. The average is about fifty-five years, to which years can be added or subtracted for mitigating factors such as childhood and substance-abuse issues, criminal history, and the brutality of the crime.

On August 22, there was little about the sentencing in the local media.

Despite the significance of the day for a select few close to both Sarah and her victims, there were bigger stories with local ties. United Airlines, a significant local employer, was cutting jobs, and a police union was making noise about money.

So, in a brief hearing, Magnus-Stinson sentenced Sarah to one hundred and ten years in prison in a state where the average inmate serves about half that sentence.

"This wasn't a spontaneous event," the judge said, as Sarah sobbed openly. "This was a plan and she was with Richard Hull every step of the way."

With some good time breaks in there, Sarah could expect to serve fifty years, making her seventy-three years old when she would be released.

Even as Sarah contended that she didn't pull the trigger that October evening two years before, it never mattered. Sells had convinced the jury that without Sarah, there would have been no murder.

"It did not matter who pulled that trigger as long as they were both there; they were both culpable," Sells says. "It was a plan on the part of both of them. And the judge felt that Sarah was the influence, the one who really caused it to happen. That it was her Charles Manson influence and manipulation that caused it to occur."

Had the victims been average people without a history in crime, rather than street-level criminals, Sarah and Richard would have faced the death penalty, which was relatively rare in Indiana. At the time of Sarah's trial, nine people had been put to death by lethal injection since the death penalty had been brought back as a punishment in 1977. Such a sentence was a remote possibility since at least one of the aggravating factors that would allow such a punishment was in play, that being that the crime was committed as part of a multiple murder.

Andrew Cataldi and Tricia Nordman were hardly innocent victims, and it was hard to generate a lot of sympathy for their fate. But Sells still managed to do so and elicited such sympathy from a jury.

"I don't moralize cases," Sells says. "A lot of the cases I handled didn't have innocent victims, quote unquote. But they didn't deserve to be blown apart by a 12-gauge shotgun and stuffed in a Dumpster like trash. They were druggies and had their problems with the law, but they weren't out killing people.

"If they had been innocent victims, then Richard and Sarah would have been looking at the death penalty."

Sarah has her own version of what kind of justice Sells was pushing.

"I believe Larry Sells did what he thought was best," Sarah says. "Even if he was wrong, I don't begrudge his job. We are all fallible, and in his position, that leads to two things: either freeing a guilty person or stealing a life from an undeserving person. I imagine his heart must be pretty hardened in order to shoulder that responsibility. It still doesn't change the fact that he prosecuted me for things I should not have been accountable for."

———

Pender would appeal for years, until she had exhausted every avenue of hope. One of her chief contentions was that her lawyer, James Nave, the former prosecutor turned public defender, was inept. It's a traditional complaint, one heard in prisons all over the United States, Monday-morning quarterbacking, with the big game lost and no more Sundays left.

"My attorney did an inadequate job of defense; there were many times I wanted to fire him, stand up and defend myself," she says. "I am convinced I would have done a better job. If not, at least I could only blame myself."

Sarah continued her letter writing. In a note sent to her former boss, John Most, between her trial and her sentencing, she thanked him for attending the trial and allowed that she was shocked that the jury had come back with a guilty verdict.

Sarah already had it planned that the next meeting with her ex-boss would be over a celebratory lunch, toasting freedom. Instead, she said the trial was a disaster, complete with "planted evidence, a false witness, a crooked cop and evidence [that] was omitted. . . . Things will come to light."

In a letter to another former colleague at Most, Leo DeHerdt, the company's controller, Sarah said that the letter that was allegedly written by her to Hull, the one that played a strong role in her conviction, was a forgery that Hull set up a long time ago. She didn't know who wrote it but said, "This jail is full of criminals who have been doing this stuff for years."

She denied ever talking about her case with Floyd Pennington and told DeHerdt that the system was a corrupt pay-for-play scam, more about rules and politics than justice. "And whoever can manipulate the system better, gets the cash."

In a 2003 appeal, she said she was denied counsel at a "critical stage of her proceedings, namely, during her conversation with Pennington at Wishard."

She claimed that Pennington's testimony violated Sarah's Sixth Amendment rights, to be confronted with the witnesses against the accused. Nave also failed to do his own analysis of the letter allegedly written by Sarah in which she virtually confesses. And the testimony of Pennington—his credibility aside—went without objection despite the notion that "a criminal defendant's right to counsel is violated when the government intentionally creates a situation likely to induce that defendant to make an incriminating statement in the absence of counsel."

The Indiana Court of Appeals denied that claim, stating that "Pender has failed to establish that the state intentionally created" that situation.

In her appeal, Sarah also stated that the trial court made a mistake in failing to instruct the jury that in order to convict her, she must have specifically intended to induce Hull to kill Cataldi and Nordman. The court noted that "Pender did not object to any jury instructions at trial."

The court also ruled that the jury instructions Sarah claimed were not given applied only to cases of attempted murder.

Although Sarah's appeals were denied, in this case, even the competition acknowledges that Nave was in the weeds on the case.

"I think James kind of dialed it in on that," Sells said. And Sarah was done, for now.

Nave refused to be interviewed for this book about his work on the case.

Hammerle, the defense attorney initially hired by Roland Pender, watched from afar as things unfolded exactly as he had predicted.

"Tragically, she was never as smart as she thought she was," Hammerle says. "There is something in that double homicide. For all the sexism in our society that plays to a woman's disadvantage, the one place a woman does have an edge is in the criminal justice system. Prosecutors will go to the female first to see if they can negotiate. It all looked like he was the prime mover, and her crime was being in love with him, and she had this horrid momentary lapse of reason. And the evidence did not strongly contradict this. This intelligent young woman ended up momentarily in some kind of Bonnie-and-Clyde type thing.

"In a case like this, the one thing I am going to do is tell my client not to talk to anyone in jail. You may meet people you like, but no one is your friend. Someone is going to tell in exchange for help. But despite all advice and her intelligence, she ignored my advice and engaged in conduct she was warned not to engage in. She thought she was smarter than everyone else and could manipulate everyone in jail. I genuinely liked her."

———

Even as she was sentenced to prison for what would likely be the rest of her life, Sarah could not stop her letter writing. On September 6, 2002, two weeks after her sentencing from Judge Magnus-Stinson, Sarah wrote to the judge from the Indiana Women's Prison intake unit, where she was being processed for entry into the system.

Sarah was unhappy that she would not be serving her time there at the aged prison located just off downtown

Indianapolis but rather was being considered for incarceration at Rockville.

In a two-page letter, Sarah said she feared going to Rockville, where she would be in with the general population. Her concern was for her safety and what she believed was her notoriety. Sarah was indeed a big presence, and now, given her prison time, she feared she would have tough girls bent on making a name for themselves by taking out a popular inmate.

"I'm pleading with you to help me because I am afraid I have a one-hundred-and-ten-year sentence for a high profile double murder case and going to a huge prison with women who know intimate details about my case scares me to death," Sarah wrote. "I already have a horrible life sentence as punishment. Please do not punish me further by sending me to Rockville now. I don't know if I can deal with it."

By the end of the month, Sarah was on a bus for Rockville.

———

The murder charge, the jailing of his daughter, and the prolonged legal struggle and its setbacks took a toll on Roland Pender. He grew restless and anxious. One day, he appeared at his stepbrother's place in Lincoln, Illinois. He needed something new. Tony Culp was an instructor at the Midwest School of Welding and Technology, teaching welding for heating and air-conditioning systems.

"I talked him into taking the EPA test to become familiar and be licensed as a welder for these systems,"

Culp said. The test, part of certification, is a requirement
by the Environmental Protection Agency to ascertain a
proficiency in handling sensitive chemicals like refriger-
ants. Roland passed with the highest grade of any of
Culp's students after studying just one night. He would
begin his foray into a new industry where he would
again find financial success, just as he found it in con-
veyance systems.

There was more change wrought by Sarah's situation.

"I think that situation with Sarah is what broke up
Roland and Sheryl," Culp says. "I know Roland was so
concerned, and I am just not sure about Sheryl. She had
a son and a daughter. I can see a conflict that was there."

Roland and Sheryl divorced shortly after Sarah was
sentenced.

———

In January 2003, Richard Hull pleaded guilty to both
murders, avoiding a trial. Under a plea agreement, the
maximum he could receive was ninety years. The court
initially sentenced him to seventy-five years—sixty-five
on each count with ten years of the second count to run
concurrent with the first.

"He picked a man's gun to do a coward's deed," Sells
told the local newspaper at the time of the first sentencing. "Here's a guy that's 290 pounds—he's big enough
to go bear hunting with a switch—and he wasn't man
enough to challenge Andrew Cataldi hand-to-hand."

Sells went on to say that the evidence showed that

Cataldi was on his knees, likely begging for mercy, when the fatal shot was fired.

"The city's a whole lot safer without either Sarah Pender or Richard Hull in it," Sells said.

Hull's defense attorney, Kay Beehler, continued to claim that Hull was not the triggerman. While her client pleaded guilty—and being present at the murder and helping dispose of the bodies are still enough to warrant the murder conviction—she said that the evidence pointed to Pender as the executioner.

"Mr. Hull made the decision to take responsibility for what was his part in this horrible tragedy," Beehler said. "Mr. Hull has never denied he played a part of it. He was not a major player."

In June 2003, Hull filed an affidavit on Sarah's behalf, claiming he was the triggerman.

"On the day of October 24, 2000, I was the one who shot and killed Andrew Cataldi and Trish Nordman," Hull said in his statement. "Sarah J. Pender did not commit this crime. She did not print the letter which I have to my lawyer Jennifer M. Lukemeyer. Sarah was set up by me. I had [inmate] Steve Logan print the letter while we were in the same block together at the Marion County Jail. I did this so I could get a good plea. She did not know that this was going to happen. I have been carrying this burden for some time now, I would like to make right on the wrongs that have been done to Ms. Pender . . . The only reason she was with me after the crime was because she was scared for her life."

Sarah's appeal based on the affidavit was denied.

But in a poorly chosen appeal, Hull went back a year later, in 2004, and the appellate court found that Hull's statement on behalf of Pender constituted perjury and increased his sentence from seventy-five to ninety years.

And that is how things would stay for some time.

CHAPTER 6

Driving down the country road away from Rockville Correctional Facility, Sarah realized that her freshly minted freedom still needed some work. It was August 4, 2008, and her crafty plan of prison escape had worked. But now what?

Sarah Pender may have shucked her inmate uniform, but she was still an inmate, and with prison escape came responsibility. Evidence of that came with a phone call as Sarah and Jamie Long approached Indianapolis. Sarah's cell phone—smuggled into the prison for her by the rogue guard, Scott Spitler—startled her with its buzz.

"I'm out of work and wanted to see where you were," a man's voice said. It was Spitler.

"I'm near Indianapolis, and I can't believe I am out," Sarah said, trying to conceal her glee. She had to play it smooth. After all, she had promised Spitler $15,000 for helping her escape.

"Everything's cool," Sarah said. "Just give me six weeks to get everything settled and I'll start sending you your money."

"All right," Spitler said. "You better, because I'll tell you something, if you don't I will track down every person you know and love and I will hurt you and I will hurt them."

"I understand," Sarah said.

Being free wasn't going to come without some trouble to navigate, she realized. But while prison officials were bumbling around, trying to find out who the missing inmate was, Sarah was being shuffled from Long's Oldsmobile into another vehicle, just in case someone had made the rattletrap that was the escape vehicle. Jamie's husband, Larry, had brought his Jeep to Irving Circle Park, not far from the east-side home that he and Jamie lived in. Jamie got out and drove the Jeep, while Larry took the Oldsmobile escape vehicle away, taking it eventually to Jamie's parents' home outside of town.

From Irving Circle Park, Jamie took Sarah to a house on Brookville Road, a place that Larry was working on in his capacity as a home rehabber.

"It was a place where a lady, a pack rat to the highest extreme, had lived," Sarah said. The house was not done, and mounds of stuff—clothing, boxes of items, magazines, refuse of all kinds—were stacked up all over the place. The house was about five miles from Larry and Jamie's.

Larry and Jamie had spent the last twenty years together. She was a cleaning lady when they met in the 1980s, and Larry was a maintenance man, eighteen years her senior. Together, they had a twelve-year-old son, but Jamie's drinking had taken its toll and led her to a number of jail stays. Larry had borne the brunt of child rearing with few legal scrapes. And now, here he was, abetting a major prison escape.

Jamie left Sarah with some necessary items—a change of clothes, an inflatable mattress, a flashlight, a new pre-paid cell phone—then left to get a few more items at the CVS drugstore on East 10th Street, a few blocks away.

But Jamie was a cop magnet right now. As she returned to her home first, to check on Larry, three officers from the Department of Correction were trailing her. The officers cruised to her neighborhood, near the house in which Sarah was hiding at the time. They saw Jamie walking down East 10th Street near the CVS, a block away. They lit her up and shook her down.

"I don't know what you are talking about," Long barked at them, holding a bag containing candy and pre-paid cell phones, like the ones that Spitler had smuggled for the Rockville girls. Chagrined, the officers left. Had they simply followed her for a few more minutes, she would have walked them to the escaped murderer. Until her capture, it was as close as anyone would get to catching Sarah.

"If she hadn't been stopped . . . she would have led them right to me," Sarah said later.

When Jamie called and told Sarah of the brush with the overzealous cops, Sarah realized she had to move.

"They are on me," Jamie said with resignation.

"That's cool, I understand," Sarah replied, already armed with an alternative plan. She dialed up Peggy Darlington, known as Daisy when she was serving a term for three forgery convictions at Rockville.

Sarah first met Darlington when they were both jailed in Marion County in early summer 2001, and the older Darlington, at thirty-five, was a sounding board and older sister to Sarah, who was twenty-two. While Sarah taught Darlington to play Euchre, the older inmate imparted wisdom about her own follies—Darlington had three children, and she was on her way to prison. There were some hard roads, and Darlington had managed to take a few.

The two moved from county lockup to Rockville, and Darlington and her mother befriended Sarah over the years, writing letters and making occasional visits after Peggy was released. Darlington's mother kept a picture of Sarah around the house. But even she couldn't know about Sarah's location now that Sarah was free, lest she be one more target for the team searching for the escapee.

Peggy was at her sister's when she got the call from Sarah.

"I need you to come and get me," Sarah said. There was a tinge of panic in her voice. Peggy had already heard of the escape, which was featured on the local evening newscasts. By midnight, Sarah was sitting in the living room of Peggy's sister's home, where there was a small group of people drinking and smoking, a small Monday-night party to ease the way into the workweek. But the crew gathered at the sister's house had no idea who Sarah was. As far as they were concerned, she was just another friend over for the festivities.

"[Peggy's] brother-in-law is a cop, so of course she can't tell her family that she is helping me," Sarah said. "I slept upstairs, and I realize that everybody is calling everybody else about the escape. 'Sarah's broken out of prison, has she called you yet?' is what they were asking each other."

In fact, Sarah had ensconced herself in a cocoon of ex-con pals who were providing her with money, cell phones, shelter, and clothes, all as she moved from point to point in the Indianapolis area. She called several friends in the area, ex-cons and relatives of inmates.

Sarah called Pam Grider, the mother of one of her Rockville girlfriends, Kimberly Stull. It was a mistake; Grider immediately panicked and told her not to contact her.

"I didn't want you wrapped up in anything and I'm really sorry. I won't call you again," Sarah promised.

"That was hard for KP because she really wanted to know how things were going," Sarah said.

She next called her mom in Bradenton, Florida.

"Mom, I'm out and safe. I love you but it may be a month before I can talk to you again," Sarah told her mother, Bonnie Prosser, in a call the night after the break-out. "Look, I am fine, I have a place to stay, I have food,

I have clothes . . . Mom, I'm OK. Just call Dad and let him know I am OK too."

Bonnie broke into tears.

"Be careful and I love you," Bonnie said before the call ended, unmercifully brief.

Finally, she called Rick Hull, her partner in the crime and former boyfriend.

"I'm out," Sarah said, almost bragging. Hull was not amused. He got the call on his own contraband cell phone in his cell.

"Are you crazy?" Hull said. "They are going to trace that phone you are calling and they are going to come get both you and me."

"Oh, well, OK . . ." Sarah said. She was stoned already, Hull realized. Not a good move when you have most of law enforcement in an entire state on your heels.

"You know that all of your friends are on lockdown right now or being followed," Hull continued. It wasn't registering with Sarah. The call lasted three minutes before Sarah told Hull she had to go.

They both hung up. Shortly after the call, Department of Correction agents came out to Pendleton Correctional Facility and shook down Hull's cell. They found a phone. Those things cost $400 in prison. Sarah's urge to brag cost Hull.

It would be this way for some time, with Sarah making calls to old friends and family, sometimes at previously arranged times and on phones that were purchased expressly for that one call, then disposed of.

Any more than one call from a store-bought phone could be traced by her pursuers, which, starting on Tuesday, August 5, was a team composed of officers from the U.S. Marshals' office, the state police, and Indiana Department of Correction cops. The team members put taps on the phones of suspected Pender friends and family. Incoming calls over a period of time would allow them to sit and wait. Once a call came in, tracing technology allowed them to find that originating cell phone tower, giving a locale that could be very specific. Sarah was aware of this and took pains to avoid making more than one call from any area and from any one phone.

Sarah would soon make the esteemed U.S. Marshals' 15 Most Wanted list, a five feet eight, 150-pound—her weight was listed a bit lower than where she actually tipped the scale—double murderer who was determined, according to a wanted poster, to be "armed and dangerous," with a reward of up to $25,000 for information leading to her capture.

The search for escapees and other fugitives in Indianapolis often fell to an Indiana State Police investigator named Ryan Harmon, a thirty-six-year-old law enforcement veteran and married father of two who defined his job duties as "hunting mankind." He worked as part of a cooperative agreement between the state and federal agencies, and both got a good deal on him.

His eleven years in justice began with road patrol of

Indiana's 157-mile toll road, where he developed a keen sense of which speeding vehicle would be carrying drugs. His success in drug interdiction earned him a promotion into white-collar crime investigations—including the thankless job of obtaining arrests related to felonies committed by government officials and fellow cops—on up to an FBI task force position, and in 2007 into his current position with the U.S. Marshals Service. At six feet four and 250 pounds, Harmon's size is as impressive as his resume, and his colloquial, gee-whiz demeanor belies an ability to track and find the bad guys. Harmon's ability to be truly concerned with the dilemma faced by a criminal, that of right or wrong, enabled him to capture rapists, con artists, burglars, and murderers over the years, and he took the Pender case with trademark inquisitiveness.

"To capture her, I would have to think like her, and to do that, I would have to know everything I could about her," Harmon says. To gain that insight into Sarah's head and the type of people who might help her, Harmon paid a visit to Jamie and Larry Long on the Tuesday following the escape. As Sarah was moving around town, Harmon was making friends with the Longs.

He drove to their house, knocked on the door, and when he entered, he let them know the story.

"I'm not DOC," he said in a steady, no-bullshit voice. "Now shut up; don't talk. You have one option: Tell me where she is."

The couple cringed. Harmon had scared them. He

looked at the wall, at a picture of Larry Long, in his Vietnam military attire.

"You a vet?" Harmon asked Larry.

"Yessir, I am," Larry replied.

"I think that's great, and I appreciate that," Harmon came back. "I want to work with you. I don't want you to go to jail. You have a son, don't you?"

Larry nodded. Jamie looked blank.

"Let's do this right, let's find Sarah," Harmon urged.

With Larry now feeling some camaraderie with the agent, he looked to Jamie.

She agreed to help. And that help started with a lie— she said she had dropped Sarah at Southern Plaza, south of the city, and that somehow Sarah had moved herself to a rural hiding place.

Harmon had to believe her at this point, at least a little. Would she deceive him right out of the gate, blatantly and in front of her husband? Maybe, but Harmon pushed Jamie and asked her to call Sarah.

She did just that, putting the cell phone on speaker, so that Harmon could listen.

"Country life is great," Sarah told Jamie. "I think I'm something like forty-five miles away. I just had a great breakfast."

It was code, Harmon says. Somehow in the conversation, there were cues that alerted Sarah that Jamie had been compromised.

"I knew it at the time, or I felt it," Harmon says. "They had somehow rehearsed this kind of thing. But I didn't

want to say anything in case they were going to give
some clues in the conversation that I could actually
break, a code I could understand."

Sarah was actually ten minutes away, stashed at
Peggy Darlington's sister's house. These cons had their
game down.

————

Harmon was somewhat hamstrung in terms of evidence
collecting and source gathering because of some of the
politics at work at the beleaguered Indiana Department of
Correction and the Parke County Sheriff's office. He was
working Jamie for information, and Jamie, despite her ob-
fuscation, seemed willing to help in some way. But the
Department of Correction had already arrested the guard,
Scott Spitler, and he had rolled on Jamie Long. And the
DOC wanted to arrest Long immediately in order to save
what face it had left after their public embarrassment. The
investigation was usually a joint effort between several
agencies, but a jailbreak generally fell to agents from the
U.S. Marshals' office and the Department of Correction.
Harmon led the case now and wanted to work Long for as
much info as he could get. The DOC wanted to put Long
behind bars right away, where she would likely clam up
on Harmon. There were politics to be played, and the state
wasn't about to have a hotshot detective screw that up.
Harmon was aware of the time element and that Jamie's
days of freedom were about to end.

Two days after his initial visit, on August 7, Harmon
pulled his battered, police-issued Ford Taurus up to the

Long home, on Ninth Street. It was around noon. Jamie was alone, and she came out to the porch to meet the detective.

"Listen, we can use your help; they know you are the one who drove her off," Harmon said. "What can we do here?"

"You aren't asking the right questions," Jamie replied. "I'm not lying, though."

Then she gave it up. To start with, she went inside and fetched two boxes of personal effects that Sarah had sent to Jamie from the prison on July 21, 2008, two weeks ahead of her escape. The boxes held meter-stamped envelopes along with letters, pictures, journals, essays, and contact information for friends, which together provided a snapshot of just who Sarah was and what circle of friends and allies she might have gathered in the wake of her escape.

Jamie also handed over a number of money orders, some blank, some made out to her, some to her husband, Larry.

"I'm the postmaster," Jamie said. "The money that Sarah needs for her run is right here. This is it. When those drugs are sold in the prison, the money comes from the outside to me. I then send a cut to Spitler and keep the rest for Sarah."

And that was it. As Harmon and Jamie stood on that porch in the benign little working-class neighborhood on a warm, sunny weekday afternoon around 3 p.m., a cadre of police officers pulled up to the house in three cars, guns drawn. Jamie surrendered with a small smile.

For her role in the escape, Long received the maximum, seven years, for aiding an escape.

As she was led out of the courthouse several days after being arraigned, a TV reporter accosted the shackled Long, clad in gray-and-white prison stripes.

"Why did you help Scott out? Do you regret it?" the reporter asked, referring to Scott Spitler, the prison guard who worked with Jamie to traffic drugs in and out of Rockville.

"Why don't you get the fuck out of my face?" Long shot back.

Sarah says she thought Jamie would get maybe a couple of years, up to four at the most. But the maximum sentence shows just how angry the prison system was about this.

"She said I deserve to be happy," Sarah said. "She said that if she could do twenty years of my time, she would."

———

Scott Spitler most likely did not share Jamie Long's munificence regarding prison-break information. He talked but didn't tell investigators much, and Harmon never even bothered to talk with him.

Charged with aiding escape and trafficking with an inmate, the fallen guard was officially a pauper according to the definition given by the Parke County court system. His court-appointed lawyer, James Bruner, stated quickly that his client was ready to take a deal. Spitler made his first court appearance, without a lawyer, the Friday after

Sarah's escape. The court entered a plea of not guilty on his behalf and set bond at $50,000. The usual 10 percent for bail was not allowed.

The case against Spitler was solid. Sarah was seen on the antiquated video surveillance system in street clothes walking toward the fueling areas for facility vehicles. A check of the security gate log showed that three vehicles had been to the fueling area around that time. Spitler was one of the drivers.

"Spitler and Pender were known associates outside the realm of normal correctional officer/offender interactions prior to this date," according to a probable cause affidavit filed with the court by the state. "Spitler was also suspected of trafficking and unprofessional conduct with offenders."

The affidavit also notes that Spitler admitted bringing Benadryl and "other drugs" into the prison for Pender and that sometimes more than 100 pills were moved in at a time. He also said he got Sarah a cell phone so the two could maintain contact. Sarah had promised him $15,000 for helping her escape, Spitler told the investigators.

"Spitler stated that he had discussed the escape with his wife because they needed the money and that she had told him not to do it."

On February 17, 2009, Spitler pleaded guilty to aiding escape, and the trafficking with an inmate charge was dropped by agreement.

Despite his egregious crime, Spitler had his supporters, mostly family. As sentencing approached, his brother,

Robert Spitler II, sent an e-mail to the judge, Samuel Swaim, and asked for some leniency.

"I am one of five siblings of Scott's and I know Scott has complete remorse for the crime he committed . . . I feel he has served his time in the Rockville Jail."

A sister, Rondo Jo McCullough, also wrote the judge, casting Sarah as some kind of leader, complete with acolytes.

"I feel Scott would never have been involved in this whole mess had he felt his family had not been in danger due to the threats that were given to him by Sarah Pender and her followers."

Another sister, Cheryl Messer, wrote that "I feel that Sarah Pender, being compared to Charles Manson by her last prosecuting attorney, saw his depression and played on his emotional state of mind at that time. Also knowing now the huge network of friends inside and outside the facility that she has would scare me as well."

Spitler received seven years, with a projected release date of February 2012. Perhaps in a show of solidarity among law enforcement officers, though, Spitler began serving his sentence in the county jail across the street from Rockville, where doing time is much easier than in a state facility. In most states, dirty cops and wayward prison guards are placed in protective custody at state prisons for such serious crimes. He was eventually moved to Miami Correctional Level 3 Facility in Kokomo, Indiana, the state's largest prison.

Ryan Harmon examined the contents of the boxes that Long turned over to him in hopes it would give him an idea of just how smart his quarry was. He found the detritus of a conflicted life, of an incarcerated young woman who was receiving plenty of love and support from the outside, and of a girl with dreams and hopes.

It was not a snapshot; it was a long-form biography. Harmon dug in, learning about this person he was devoting his life to catching.

A birthday card from her mother, Bonnie, offered hope: "If God has a plan, maybe we will be together soon. Close your eyes and think of me giving you a big hug."

A letter dated May 20, 2005, from Bonnie reads: "I just want to tell you that I love you so much. Your letters have helped me so much . . . I can't tell you how much you mean to me. When we are together I will make you your favorite cake and we will pig out. Love, Mom."

Her father, Roland, tries to encourage her in the wake of a legal setback regarding her final state appeals process in July 2006: "Keep praying what God's plan is for you. I always believed there is a plan and it includes you."

Roland calls attention to Sarah's biggest mistake: the constant letter writing as she awaited trial and her attorney tried to secure a deal for her.

"You would have behaved differently before the trial," Roland said. He promised that God would deliver her from prison. And just in case, Roland told her he had given a new lawyer a $1,000 retainer to begin work on her next appeal.

"I believe in you," Roland told her.

A month later, he tells Sarah in a note dated August 5, 2006, that her sister got a divorce and that he sold his truck. He added: "Reminder to you that all things are possible through prayer and forgiveness. Sarah, I love you, Dad."

In other notes, Roland tells of whitewater rafting trips and motorcycle rides. Another in 2003 comes from Zimbabwe. One he signs, "I love you and am proud of you."

A list—Sarah liked to compile lists—provides an optimistic look to the future; she lists the things she wants to do in her life before she dies, including meet NASCAR race driver Ryan Newman, make an album, snorkel the Great Barrier Reef, learn to drive a speedboat, take a train to Chicago for dinner, catch a home-run baseball, sing the national anthem at a NASCAR race, fall in love, and run a 10K.

Another reads in simple statements her belief in God, her love of "transparent people," and her wish to "grow up" to be a stock-car racing engineer.

She also made goals with consideration for her prison life, things like use the library twice a month, make the weekly church choir practice, exercise four times a week, and "promote green energy/recycling within facility."

Sarah wrote a song she titled "Your Light," wrote an essay on a miscarriage that may or may not have been hers, and put together an essay on the politics of NASCAR.

Other writings included an informed critique of "Sonny's Blues," a 1957 short story by James Baldwin, and notes for an oral report on Anton LaVey, founder and high priest of the Church of Satan.

There are communications with suitors on the outside, including frequent visitor and pen pal Arthur Ford, son of Art Ford, a legend in New York–area broadcasting for his *Art Ford's Jazz Party*, a late-1950s TV show whose guests included Les Paul. Ford adored Sarah in his letters and made several trips from his New York home to see her.

Another admirer, from California, outlined his own legal theories; then, aware of Sarah's interest in physics, he attempted to woo her with some geek talk: "You asked about piezoelectric effect. The physical dimensions of certain crystals change in the presence of an electric field."

Marvin in Bloomington just wanted to let her know he cared.

One letter from Hull remained in her stash, dated October 29, 2007, in which he states, "I lost my temper . . . because of some of my past actions, I lost my two best friends," apparently referring to Andrew Cataldi and Sarah.

Her father wrote her a letter dated June 8, 2008, less than two months before her escape.

"Really enjoyed our visit," he wrote. "So much to talk about, an exciting future for both of us ahead . . . know that whatever decision you make, I will love you. I understand the crossroads you are at."

And the pictures. It is quickly apparent that Sarah is a

visual documentarian. She keeps handwritten notes scribbled on torn and frayed bits of paper as well as pictures that may or may not tell a story. She stands with family friends, her sister, father, mother, Jamie Long, and even the dogs she trained. Especially the dogs, actually. Golden retrievers who grin into the camera with that trademark candor, smiling just as broadly as Sarah. In one photo, she hugs her father, Roland, as he smiles widely. In another, Sarah sits between two retrievers, beaming in a royal-blue prison-issue smock and khakis, while the dogs beam their beauty at the lens.

Arthur Ford looks for all the world a smitten, mustached young man in wire-framed glasses and a maroon knit sweater hugging Sarah in a photo dated May 14, 2005.

Also in the box, keepsakes in Sarah's eyes, are notes from other inmates, flirty missives inviting her to have sex and some naked shots of former inmates now on the outside.

All the letters, along with the case file, gave Harmon an idea that he was up against one of the more formidable foes he had yet to encounter. She was smart and she was streetwise. The case would keep him running nonstop for the next 135 days, taking him from Seattle, Washington, where he would sit down with Sarah's father, to Washington, D.C., where he would tape an episode of *America's Most Wanted*, and out to Rockville Correctional Facility thirty-five times.

"We got a bead on her right away, but there was an amazing underground that she had already built up before her break," Harmon says. He choked off $1,700 almost immediately after her escape by grabbing those money orders sent to Jamie Long and intended for Sarah to help her in her flight.

"We got all kinds of information, but she had really planned this out. And it made for a very difficult track."

——— ——

Sarah had been counting on that cutoff $1,700 that Harmon intercepted as a stake to launch her new life, money she had earned through selling drugs in the prison via an intricate web spun by herself; the guard Spitler, who was now blabbering like a little girl caught skipping school; and Jamie Long. Some of that money had come through the prison, an avenue that was quickly closed off through a search of mail coming into Long's house.

But before her arrest, Jamie gave Sarah $200, which was transferred between Peggy Darlington and Jamie at a quick meeting at a McDonald's early on the morning of August 5. During the meeting, Sarah, still in desperate fear that cops were following Jamie, hid in the trunk of Peggy's car.

"Jamie [went] into the McDonald's, [got] some food [and] sat down and Peggy would come in and get something and whenever [Jamie] saw Peggy, she would go to the bathroom and drop off the money and [Peggy] would follow behind her, pick it up and bring it out to me," Sarah said. Along with the cash was a new prepaid cell phone and a phone card. Sarah had begun by sitting in Peggy's car, waiting.

"But I didn't know, what if they're following them? I don't want to be sitting out in the car . . . so I climbed in the trunk; she had a little, a car where the seats fold down. So that kinda sucked."

From the McDonald's, Peggy took Sarah to a Motel 6 on Shadeland Avenue on the city's northeast side. The area was familiar to Sarah; the house in which she had grown up was only three miles from the motel. Sarah peeled $50 from the roll of cash Peggy had received from Jamie and waited in the car for Peggy to get a room. She asked that it be on the second floor.

"Don't worry about me, I'll be OK," Sarah said, as the two walked up the stairs. The two of them carried bags; some grocery items, toiletries, and hair dye. In the room, Sarah embarked on her first meager attempt at disguise.

"Once I got up there I dyed my hair . . . really dark brown," Sarah said. "Right before I left prison I cut my hair and stretched it curly and up, then when I got [to the motel room], I cut it up to my shoulders."

One call Sarah made the morning of the money drop was to Thea Fisher, a forty-three-year-old part-time hooker who had served some time with Sarah at Rockville on a cocaine charge. For a long time Thea had been aware of Sarah's desire to escape from Rockville, with Sarah directly telling her that it was going to happen one day.

"I told her, 'One day I'm not going to be able to take this anymore and I'm going to have to get out. And I

know that I can escape' and that's why I never put Thea
on my visitor or phone list," Sarah said. "I told her
[long ago] that I would need ID and would ask for her
help."

Fisher, also known as Linny, was used to hearing the
bluster of almost every convict. A lot of people talk shit
about busting out, like they watched *The Great Escape*
or *Birdman of Alcatraz* or *The Shawshank Redemption*
too many times. But with Sarah, well, she wasn't a physics major at Purdue for nothing.

Thea most recently had been working at a strip joint
for a while, then dabbling in bartending, then turning
occasional tricks while living with a man on the city's
west side.

"Basically, she was mooching off guys," Sarah said.
"She had a couple of sugar daddies."

As Sarah prepared to be picked up at the Motel 6 by
Fisher, Ryan Harmon was already at the Pendleton Correctional Facility, thirty miles northeast of Indianapolis.
His visit was to Rick Hull, the hulking convict who had
sold his soul for Sarah. Hull was beefed up like a bison
on steroids, a behemoth of a man who now had plenty of
time to spend honing his body, the one asset that God
had doled out to him. "I was putting two and two together pretty quick, since I had choked off that money,"
Harmon says. "I knew she was going to be hurting for
money. And Rick told me that she would probably be
doing something sexual for money. And he also knew
that Sarah would be in touch with Thea."

As Harmon left Pendleton, he decided to head over to Club Venus, a squalid strip joint on Sixteenth Street over by the Indianapolis Motor Speedway, which had once employed Thea. If the facade of the Venus was crumbling, the interior was a red-light nightmare of dilapidation. Three name changes over the years didn't change the fact that it was a strictly low-rent place, nestled as it was among pawnshops, loan-shark operations, and fast-food joints. Harmon was not crazy about stopping by. He had already been told by several sources that Sarah would turn to sex in order to make some fast money. And this was the fastest, for sure.

As he neared Club Venus, though, a Crime Stoppers tip came across the radio—the first of thousands of calls that would be fielded in the coming months. The tip was for a place on the east side, close to Harmon's location. He had to check it out. It took up an hour of valuable time and bore nothing. This was how it was going to be, he thought. For a man like Harmon, accustomed to free-flowing tips when he usually did his searches, these were coming in spare and random, and without leading to anything. Sarah was not going to be an easy catch, he feared.

————

Thea took Sarah back to her house, again a place bustling with various players of sketchy character. Sarah and Thea cooked dinner, and Sarah helped with some house-cleaning. She handed over some money for food and gas.

"By this time, I'm down to like $100 . . . I'm thinking 'I gotta get some money' . . . and I gotta figure out what I'm gonna do. And I had a couple of different options I was going to work with, but I figured I needed to be as independent as possible, and I also have to get the fuck out of here. And then Thea said, 'Well, I have an idea.'"

CHAPTER 7

—

Tom Welch is a weak man.

He'll be the first to tell you this, outlining his various addictions. In the summer of 2008, it was sex, but in the past it had been gambling, and even alcohol back in his youthful days.

Meeting Ashley Thompson, though, was a turning point in his life. August 6, 2008—he won't forget it. Maybe it was even the first step on his way to true happiness, he thought. She was an overtly sexual and flirtatious woman, with an agreeable, sunny disposition, who was a few days shy of her thirtieth birthday when Welch met her at the dilapidated Budget Inn and Fantasy Suites, a two-story no-tell motel behind the El Rodeo Mexican restaurant just off Interstate 74 on the city's west side. It has since closed, but in 2008, the Budget Inn was one more rogue's motel within earshot of the superhighway, with fraying, dirty drapes in the rooms and a chipping exterior of beige paint.

Ashley's story was a tough one; her abusive cop husband was chasing her down while she tried to divorce him. She was on the run. She needed a little help.

Welch was introduced to Ashley by his friend Linny, also known as Thea Fisher, a dancer at Club Venus. He had known Linny for a year or so in a somewhat traditional stripper-customer relationship. They had drinks, maybe a meal, then some sex.

"I am sure that she was not living well, and a lot of the time I would say, 'Here's $50' or 'I know you have a kid, here's $20.' I would help her with this and that," Welch said.

In recent months, Welch's sex binge had reached epic proportions at the finely attuned age of fifty-three. He could take you to five strip joints in town and be shown to his reserved seat.

Welch's wife, Marilyn, had a career on the fast track even as she reached her fifties. She had started at American Express as a reservation agent in the travel group in the late 1980s, and now she was the director of market development. It meant plenty of high-class corporate travel and a fat paycheck, which, combined with Tom's flowing riches from his own trucking firm, was making the Welches a pretty fancy couple. They were on the Dean's List at Purdue University for their generous contributions to the College of Liberal Arts. Marilyn was also on the alumni board for the college.

While she pursued her career, Tom had semi-retired

at the age of forty-seven, content to get around and enjoy the good money he had already made as co-owner of a trucking company in Indiana. He still had a hand in the operation but was more of an overseer than a day-to-day chief.

"I'm playing golf, I'm going to the casinos," Welch said. "I did it for a year or two. My golf game got into the seventies, what more can you do? I was pretty damn good."

Nothing much left to do but maybe try some sexual experimentation.

He had been asking Linny for some time to line up a threesome that he'd gladly pay for.

Now Linny had her third in Ashley Thompson. Known to the public as Sarah Pender.

————

Sarah's alias was easy to come by. She had conceived it a while back when she was preparing her escape, right down to the birth date of August 8, 1978. August 8 was her father's birthday. She took one year off of her own birth year of 1979, making her fictional character thirty years old rather than her real age of twenty-nine. And her name? It would be Ashley Thompson.

"Thea had this idea," Sarah said. "She knew this guy who had been bugging her for a threesome and so she comes to me and says 'If you want to, you can make a quick $100.' And I was like, 'I gotta do what I gotta do.' So I said 'What's he like?' And I met him and he was really decent, I really liked him . . . there are some things

I just don't do, some guys I won't touch with a ten-foot pole. But I was really pleased and I was like 'Why is this guy paying for pussy?'"

Sarah gave Tom a warm hug when they met, and the tryst went fine. When it was over, Tom looked at Sarah—Ashley, as far as he knew—and asked where she was heading.

"I'm going to get a room tonight," she said.

"Hell, I got this one [booked], and I'm leaving," Welch said.

Welch's home in the suburb of Avon was a fifteen-minute drive from the motel. Marilyn was traveling. It was an easy choice, a no-brainer some might say, to come back the next morning for breakfast. After that, the next seven hours were spent getting to know each other in the most intimate fashion. They stayed in that room for three days, mostly having sex. There was only one minor variation.

"We changed rooms because of bugs," Welch said.

———————

"Do you know who Ashley is, for real?"

Linny was dying to tell Tom that Ashley Thompson was not as she had presented herself. She told him straight up: she was, in fact, an escaped convict named Sarah Pender.

"Bullshit," Welch replied when Linny told him. Not that it would have made any difference even if it were true. He had already started having feelings for Ashley after the first twenty-four hours with her. It was August 7. Welch was already deeply involved, addicted so to speak. A fugitive? Sure, that's fine.

"The news wasn't a real stopper of conversation," Welch said.

When he and Sarah did take a break from the sex, the new couple switched on the TV. On August 8, a local news broadcast announced the arrest of Jamie Long in connection with the prison break of Sarah Pender, the convicted double murderer. Accompanying the story was a photo of Sarah taken by a friend during a visit to the prison, a becoming head shot, sans makeup, that showed her with red hair, longer, past her shoulders.

Ashley was Sarah, no doubt about that. Even Welch could see it.

"I saw that one picture and I knew it was true," Welch said. "It was just a word to me—*fugitive*. I was hooked after the first day. It was like eating Lay's potato chips; you can't have just one. When it was on the news, she said it was all bullshit talk."

"I wasn't at that murder," Sarah told him. "Rick killed them, they were in a drug partnership. I came to the house and he had killed them and he told me to get rid of them or he was going to kill me. I was twenty and stupid."

Which was fine with Welch.

Sarah had entranced him.

"I trusted her because everything I would see and hear, that wasn't the person I knew," Welch said.

For the rest of the week, Welch commuted to his lover

in the dumpy motel room he paid for. He bought her some clothes, brought her food.

"As time went by, we were getting to know each other and I'm really attracted to this guy," Sarah said. "He's smart, he runs a trucking logistics company. He was married but he was saying, 'What do I have to do to get you into my life?'"

On Saturday, August 9, Tom and Sarah emerged from their motel room, the escaped convict never seeming to mind the idea that someone, somehow, could peg her at any time. It just didn't seem possible, in fact. Welch was unfazed by the news that she was on the lam from a law enforcement cadre that included the U.S. Marshals Service.

Sarah told Welch she was innocent of the crime, and that worked just fine with him. Let's go to a casino, he proposed. Of course, she said. No worries.

They made the two-hour drive to Rising Sun, Indiana, home of the Grand Victoria Casino and Resort. Welch was a diamond player, entitling him to a free room, two free buffets a day, and pretty much anything else he needed. When they arrived, he directed his new girlfriend to the gift shop, where he bought her a small gold cross on a neck chain. That evening after dinner, they caught an Eagles impersonation band at Big Vic's Pub & Grub, the casino bar.

The bar was hardly a high-class hangout, nor was the casino anything special. But the Grand Victoria may as well have been the Bellagio for someone who only four days previously had been told when to eat, when to bathe, and when to sleep. The new world that Sarah had stepped into would have been a vast change even had she moved right from the drug house on Meikel into the arms of Tom Welch. But the new inputs—the ringing slot machines representing won riches, the tender-cut beef and seafood in one of the casino's four eateries, the people, walking around free—were all new to Sarah, who felt an appreciation for life she had never felt before.

"When you're in prison, it's a static setting; nothing ever changes," Sarah said. "When you get outside [prison], you're not taking in the external environment so you can focus on the smaller things like people or body movement, and when I was out I was like 'Wow, trees, grass, cows, oh, this is so nice.' And then when I went to the grocery store for the first time I was so overwhelmed because there were a million choices for everything, I was like 'Oh my God, how do people go to the grocery store?' It really took a while. I think it was a month before it wasn't so foreign."

When the weekend wound down, Sarah told Welch that the one thing she really wanted to do was to find a job. Her story—the cop's wife, Ashley Thompson tale—was solid, she felt, and she asked Welch for his help.

What does a Tom Welch, who survived open-heart surgery at thirty-two and made it through a nerve disorder that kept him in the hospital for nine months the prior year, do with this request?

The smitten businessman couldn't refuse.

———

Squirreling Sarah away was an immediate felony charge for Tom Welch, if he were to get caught. A man with so much to lose obviously had a debilitating dependency problem. He was a man who took his pleasures seriously and yet maintained a tie to his wife that was his life-blood; his business, GC3 Logistics, was even registered to her American Express work address in downtown Indianapolis.

But now, Welch was ready to help collude with Sarah to keep her from going back to prison.

He had enough contacts in the region for sure; Sarah had already told him that she wanted to be away from Indianapolis.

Paul Bridges could help. He was Welch's childhood pal going back to first grade. Bridges lived in central Indiana and was in the construction business and was building some apartment buildings as an add-on to an assisted-living center near Forest Park, a suburb ten miles north of Cincinnati. Bridges knew of Tom's robust fondness for girls, particularly dirty ones. The two had been talking regularly, as usual, over the past weeks, even before Sarah entered the picture. Bridges was getting ready to have hip surgery and needed some organizational help on the Ohio project before he felt he could leave the whole thing to a replacement manager who was coming in. What he needed was someone with some construction office experience.

"He told me he was looking for help, and I said 'I

have this friend named Ashley,'" Welch said. "I told him the whole story."

It was the Ashley story, though, not the fugitive story.

So it all sounded fine, except Bridges was headed home for a bit to consult with his doctor, and it might be a few days before he needed Ashley.

"I said, 'That's OK,' and I left her in Cincinnati for a week," Welch said.

Her home from the tenth to the thirteenth was the Forest Park Suites, a six-story business hotel right off Interstate 275 offering a pool, workout room, and free breakfast buffet. Next door was a Cracker Barrel, and across the major connector road, a Walmart.

The place was three miles from the work site, and it beat Rockville, for sure. By the time Bridges returned, Sarah was getting used to being free but not without the price of a general uneasiness. Would Welch turn her in? Who was this Paul, and if he were to find out the truth, would he squeal?

She had some extreme paranoia that Welch might sell her out. "I came back home and she would call me every—constant—I mean it was . . . we would talk minimally two to five times a day, and that might be on the low side. Or she might send me text messages, you know, 'How you doin'?'"

Sarah did have some leverage though: Welch's marital status and the potential felony charge Welch would face for aiding a fugitive.

When Bridges returned, on the fourteenth of August, Sarah moved into a small condominium on the work site.

It was a two-bedroom unit, with her in one bedroom and Bridges in the other. But he was gone frequently once she learned her work. Her experience at Carl E. Most & Son was handy—much of the detail was similar, from typing contracts to dealing with subcontractors. For two weeks she toiled and came back to the condo. At night, Sarah would make calls to the prepaid cell phones she had distributed around to her friends. She was smart enough to know how tracking calls went. But she made herself impossible to trace because she would make one call per phone and then discard it.

One night, she called Peggy Darlington, the ex-con who had provided her with shelter on her first night out of prison. They hadn't talked since Peggy had dropped her at the motel on Shadeland in Indianapolis. It was clear almost immediately that the cops were pressing Peggy. Sarah knew intuitively that information had been handed to the cops about her involvement in the hiding of Sarah. And she was right.

"Please turn yourself in," Peggy urged Sarah.

"No, why would I do all this to escape and start a new life and then turn myself in?" Sarah asked. Sensing Peggy's concern that Sarah had embarked on a never-take-me-alive mission, Sarah added, "I promise I won't pull a gun on the cops."

She got off the phone and pondered.

"Even if the police don't know about the phones, if she's that scared, either she's acting like that because they are threatening her or she is scared and is going to [spill]," Sarah said. "I thought, 'Maybe this isn't a good idea . . . I don't want anyone to think I am hurt or anything, but . . .' So I just said I am not going to call. I don't want to cause any more trouble than I already have for her."

The next morning at work, she went back to being Ashley Thompson, the victimized refugee on the run from her abusive cop ex-hubby. It was some serious acting. Her arrangement, struck in a deal between Welch and Bridges, was that Sarah would work in exchange for a room at the condo, some food, and Bridges's closed mouth. Welch took care of whatever needs she had in terms of clothes or accessories, sometimes leaving her $100 when he left after a visit.

For several days, Sarah worked, slept, and worked. Her routine was the stuff of quiet desperation for most people; for her, it was the sweet fruit of a massive work of manipulation and cunning that ended up with her breathing free air every morning on her walk from the condo to the trailer office on the work site.

Welch's visits were pure play for the two. Their forays into Cincinnati-area nightlife led them across the Central Bridge over the Ohio River and into Newport, Kentucky, which lures many an Ohioan to its strip joints, mostly set on Monmouth Street. The Brass Mule, also known as the Brass Ass to those familiar with the area, is an anachronism among strip joints.

One night, Sarah and Tom invited Paul to come along; maybe he could have some fun, they thought.

"We were going to get Paul laid," Sarah said. It didn't work out: "We were close to being successful. But then

Paul decides he had to go to work in the morning and it's like 1 a.m."

Bridges likely didn't care for the company he was being courted to keep. But Tom and Sarah really enjoyed the place.

"When we went there the first night . . . there was this real tall blonde there and I made out with her and she had really nice breasts and [Tom] was like 'Would you like to fuck her?' and I was like, 'Well, maybe I'm not really interested, just messing around.' But you know he was like 'I'm going to get two chicks together, this is going to be great.'"

So the two went back a second time and made it happen.

The cost was $350, slapped on Tom's credit card.

"It was an adventure," Sarah said.

On the morning of August 18, Bridges was preparing to return to Indiana for a stay at his farm outside Spiceland in the cornpone beauty of the central part of the state.

Sarah missed Welch, and her isolation continued to fuel her fear of being apprehended. And the calls to her friends, who she was now sure were being pressed by the cops, weren't helping.

So Sarah joined Bridges for the two-hour drive back to central Indiana, where Bridges stuck her in a no-tell motel room on Highway 3, the main drag of New Castle, before heading home. From here, it was Welch's problem for a few days.

Welch met her at the motel, and the two began to advance their courtship. It wasn't a problem. "We got real close," Welch said. He had grown up in the area and rarely got back there. It was a sweet return.

"I took her down to the graveyard and showed her my dad . . . she's a tremendously compassionate person."

They drove the winding highways of central Indiana with such freedom that it sometimes seemed as if Sarah's incarceration never happened. Blue skies, green grass, red barns, brown earth—all merged together as in a painting. Homes, weathered with flecking white paint, wooden and still, pocked the landscape, each offering a new story, a place where people lived free on the beautiful plains amid black-and-white cows and golden horses.

It was a world of hayrides and, soon, pumpkin patches. Sarah had returned to where she grew up, for a time, when the world was kinder to her, and she was kinder to it.

One evening, they dined at a Bob Evans Restaurant, Sarah hiding in plain sight. No one had any idea that she was the girl whose face had been plastered on local television for two weeks. Her dyed hair had already begun to turn back to its natural brown color, although it was still considerably shorter than it was in the police photos.

In the company of an older, attractive man, Sarah looked like one more love-struck woman of twenty-nine. She had thought Welch was in the midst of some midlife crisis, but it hardly mattered to her. Both of them knew she was going to return to Cincinnati, and the daylong interlude had been intense.

Reality was closing in; he wanted something more than just a token love affair. The married man bought his girlfriend a ring.

"I don't want you down there with all these guys on the worksite hitting on your ass," Welch said.

"No, I love you," Sarah came back.

He turned the car into the parking lot of Smith Jewelers, a small family-run place that had served the area for sixty years. It was a budget deal in a strip mall, enveloped by fast food and concrete, but the reputable place served a purpose. The price of Welch's devotion: $170.95.

"Now you can just tell people you're married," Welch advised.

The lovebirds headed south for the Super 8 motel in Greenfield. From there, he returned her to Cincinnati, where her paranoia would soon open the door to even more adventure on her great escape.

———

Ryan Harmon walked into Pendleton Correctional Facility ready to make a friend with a convicted murderer.

Rick Hull, expected to be locked away for the rest of his life, had little to gain by cooperating with Harmon, the detective charged with tracking down Sarah Pender. Finking on anyone was looked at as the extreme betrayal in the criminal brotherhood, something that could get a man killed, even someone as physically formidable as Hull, whose muscled girth was growing with daily access to a prison weight room. His face now sported a grizzled goatee, and his shaved head—a longtime look he never shed—still made his presence as menacing as ever.

Harmon's aim was to meet with Hull, who had called him a week or so earlier, and he hoped that he could provide insight into Sarah's habits. Hull's phone call came as little surprise to Harmon on two fronts: That Hull had a cell phone made him just like hundreds of other inmates in the Indiana Department of Correction. Cell phones were already rife under the Swiss cheese security of the state's prison system. Harmon also knew that Hull would want to see that Sarah would be apprehended safely. He still had feelings for her.

In exchange, Hull could expect very little. His ninety years were locked down, and there was no room to wriggle on that.

"I went in there knowing he had nothing to gain by helping, unless he was afraid that Sarah could get hurt," Harmon says.

And that was his plea to Hull, planned as he made the half-hour drive north to the prison, which housed close to 1,900 of the state's most violent offenders.

Harmon was already weighing a number of scenarios as to how Sarah might be surviving. Her father, Roland, was a man of means and would surely help his little girl. Roland, a fiftysomething motorcycle enthusiast and self-made man, felt the entire situation was an injustice and that his little girl was imprisoned because of the political aspirations of a few prosecutors. Sarah's mother,

Bonnie, had no money and was unlikely to be sheltering her, Harmon thought. He was also already tapping
inmates past and present at Rockville on a steady basis,
even just two weeks after the escape.

One of the first things the Indiana Department of Correction did after the escape was to place Kimmy, Sarah's
girlfriend, and Angie Stone, another conspirator in the
break, in lockdown as punishment. This took them out of
commission, unable to correspond with Sarah. Harmon
went up to Rockville and fixed that.

"Take them out, give them cell phones and let's hope
Sarah contacts them," Harmon instructed. Phone contact
would establish a call pattern, he hoped, and phones can
be traced within feet of their origin.

Now, Rick Hull was reticent but persuadable to join
the search for Sarah.

"She is too smart to be taken alive, isn't she?" Harmon asked, meeting Hull in a concrete bunker of a room
saved for lawyer visits.

Hull nodded. He never wanted to see Sarah dead,
even when she freely absolved herself of all responsibility in the crime. Hull agreed to help, only if it would save
a life. Rick Hull was no snitch; that was clear. He would
not help a cop take someone in.

But he promised to be vigilant.

"When we were out there together, she was my best
friend," Rick said. "We were together twenty-four, seven.
When she wasn't at work, she was with me."

The bond between them still existed, and Hull was
saddened by Sarah's escape when he spoke with Harmon.

"We'll probably never talk to one another again," he said. "Unless she gets caught. Then she might write me a letter."

These phones, placed by Harmon with Sarah's closest confidantes inside prison walls, even with the numbers distributed through a web of underground contacts to Sarah, would remain silent. Sarah knew what she was doing, Harmon thought. For the second time, he thought she might be out for a long time.

CHAPTER 8

For Sarah, the world was now divided into spaces where they could get you and places where they couldn't. The "they" was the cops, and after almost a month on the run, Sarah was starting to know those places. And the one place she feared most was alone. When Tom Welch was home with his wife in the Indianapolis suburbs, or running around doing God knows what, that was a bad place for Sarah's head to be. The creeping paranoia came in quickly when that happened.

Welch had been to Cincinnati twice in the two weeks she had been there, but when he left, well, the bad stuff entered her head. He left her with spending money for toiletries, extra food, whatever she might want.

But now, on September 1, the Monday that was Labor Day, her incessant phone calls and pages to Tom Welch were going unanswered and had been going straight to voice mail since Friday night. He had just returned to his home in Avon, Indiana, that evening from one more visit to see Sarah in Cincinnati, and the two-hour drive each way "wore my ass out," Welch said.

"So I didn't talk to her, but we had always talked, like every . . . she always wanted to know where I was at, what I was doing. For some reason, I was like, 'Fuck.' I didn't want to talk to her. Didn't feel like it, whatever. Well anyway, she must have gotten real panicky."

Ensconced in the middle of suburbia, an access road, and a Starbucks nightmare of big box–strip mall paranoia, Sarah picked up the phone and called Paul Bridges's home, hoping he could get ahold of Welch.

When Bridges's wife, Kimberly, answered the phone, she was surprised to hear about Sarah. Her husband had certainly never mentioned her before.

"Who is this?" Kimberly demanded.

"This is Ashley; I work for the company with Paul," Sarah came back.

When Paul got on the other line, Kimberly immediately demanded an explanation, as Sarah listened.

"What the hell is going on?" Kimberly demanded.

"This is a girl that is helping us out," Paul explained feebly.

Kimberly, a fourth-degree black-belt holder, turned her scorn on Sarah.

"I'm on my way down and you better not be there when I get there," she said.

Now Tom was getting calls from Paul Bridges as well as Sarah, both with urgent demands—handle this situation.

"What the fuck is going on with the crazy bitch?" is how Bridges asked Welch.

In addition to her fear of being discovered—maybe even the remote possibility of Welch rolling on her— "I was scared because I cared about him," Sarah said. "I was afraid that maybe something happened and he was in a hospital . . . I was also scared that maybe something happened and he was in jail."

She hadn't eaten a thing. She had tanned at a nearby tanning salon to get the tan lines Welch was, for some reason, very fond of.

But her calls still went unanswered.

To quell her fears, she sat down to write a letter to Tom, a letter that would never be sent.

"Tom—I haven't heard from you in two days. I am worried," she began. "I've been sick over it."

She at first thought she couldn't reach him because he had misplaced his cell phone. And at the same time, she wasn't about to hang around in case someone had somehow tracked her and was pressing Welch for information.

She doubted he would roll on her to the cops, and if he did, she would likely be apprehended; he knew all of her hiding spots by this time. She also allowed that she could return to her premurder lifestyle of hustling and consorting with drug dealers.

"I can, and will if I have to, but don't want to leave you," Sarah said.

She professed her love for Welch and included some telling details of her own take on the crime that got her into the situation in the first place. Sarah said she was not sorry for being caught with regard to the murders, but she was sorry that she got involved in anything like that in the first place.

"I am not sorry they are dead," Sarah wrote. "People die all the time, for lots of reasons, many at young ages . . . killing people is not such a big deal, because people die. We are human."

She outlined her case, something she had already done for Welch as the two had spent more and more time together over the previous month.

Then she addressed another issue: Welch had mentioned to her the idea of having his wife, Marilyn, killed.

"I know you think life would be easier if you killed your wife. It wouldn't. What if you do kill [Marilyn]? Don't you know what sort of pain her family will go through, especially when you quickly move on to another woman?"

Sarah moved through what would happen to him if he went through with such a horrendous act.

"If you want to keep me, then get divorced and work more days. It's a trade-off but it works a lot better than thinking you can kill people and be invincible."

She offered more advice, telling him that if he really wanted to be with her, he could cash in some assets, leave his wife, "and live middle class the rest of our lives."

Sarah ended the letter by thanking Welch "for all you have done for me, all that you have shared with me and all that you have risked to be with me . . . I have enjoyed the ride and don't ever want it to stop. Love you Tom. End of story."

That done, she began a letter to her father, Roland. She had not spoken with him since her escape but had sent him a prepaid cell phone a week or two before. But the heat she was feeling after her conversation with Peggy Darlington a week before had made her reconsider calling Roland. If the cops were to come calling and ask if he had talked with her, what would he say?

"I was not willing to compromise him," Sarah said. "Whether he would lie to me or not . . . I didn't want him to have to lie for me."

So, completing the letter to Welch, she began a letter to her father.

"Dear Dad—It has been almost a month and life is good," she typed, in another letter that was never mailed. She told him how she had a newfound appreciation for the feeling of sunshine on her skin, wearing blue jeans and sunglasses, and eating with silverware and using a stove. She told him how good it felt to take a bath, use a triple-blade razor, and have lovely scented body-wash products. Living life as a free person after all those years, she said, was almost unreal, and the smallest pleasures seemed larger than she ever recalled.

"I feel good when I watch the Food Network . . . I feel overwhelmed when I have to order stuff or shop," Sarah said. "There is just so damned much stuff."

Sarah also explained that she had sent him a phone and wanted to call him, but—considering how the police had pressed Peggy Darlington and the disturbing conversation she had that night—she thought better of it.

"I love you and am very sorry for the trouble I have caused you. Even if they never knew, I don't want to put you at any more risk."

She discussed her escape, noting that the night before her flight, she'd found nine four-leaf clovers in approximately fifteen minutes, "and I have never been able to do that."

Three psychics had told her over the years that she would be out of prison in 2008, and it had come true, Sarah told her father. And the obstacles that had befallen her in the previous couple of years, including the loss of her dog-training job over a minor infraction, developing pictures in the prison photo lab, and being put into disciplinary lockdown, were part of the process to prompt her into escape.

As the time of her escape drew near, she told her father, it became easier and easier to believe that she could pull it off. Some days, she said, she would wait with bated breath to see if that was the day. And on the days that her escape seemed more remote, she now realized, it needn't have been so discouraging.

"It was really everything I needed to get where I am right now, in order to have this second chance."

She told him that she was not crazy and had not just irrationally made a break for it. And now that she was out, she was being a good citizen free of crime.

"I even pick up litter, pull weeds, and help old people out."

She wrote of her relationship with Welch and described him as a man "I have grown to love very much . . . we are spookily made for one another." She restated some of the things she told Welch about the possible offing of his wife, cutting and pasting from one computer-written letter to the other.

"He tried to justify it by saying that it would be better for her than an embarrassing divorce, like he is trying to do her a favor. He also thinks killing off his partner in business would be a good idea. I tell him he is delusional. . . ."

Sarah also expressed some outrage for the level of public attention her escape was getting and the pressure being put on her confidantes. She said she was just living life and wished they would leave her alone.

"I know the law enforcement agencies want to make me out to be this big monster, or a female Charles Manson, or whatever. I love people, I love life. And I love to make a positive impact on them, and to get something positive from the people and environment around me."

In the letter to her father is a small handwritten note penned by Sarah: "P.S.—2 months later, everything is fine. Life is good."

Welch later told investigators that the chatter about his wife's murder "was just a conversation with a killer."

———

After hearing from Bridges of the developing drama and Sarah's conversation with Bridges's wife, Kimberly, Welch turned on his cell phone and checked the voice mail.

"If I don't hear from you in five minutes, I am on a bus," Sarah blared in her last message.

He called her. True to her word, Sarah had grabbed a cab to the bus station in downtown Cincinnati and jumped on a Greyhound. The six-hour ride was interrupted by Welch's call.

"Let me meet you," Welch said with resignation. He was going to leave again to pick up Sarah in Toledo, Ohio, a place that the two had agreed would be a fallback in the case of an emergency.

Another of Welch's seemingly endless array of buddies in the transportation business could help.

Welch called Sarah again as she sat on the bus.

"OK, stay in Toledo one night, and I'll meet you in northern Indiana and we'll head over to Chicago."

Tom's pal picked Sarah up at the bus station and shuffled her over to a hotel. The next day, he moved her to Fort Wayne, where Welch picked her up.

———

As Sarah embraced, screwed, and romanced her new boyfriend in her new life, a crew from the crime-stopping, cop-crusading TV show *America's Most Wanted* landed throughout the day at Indianapolis International Airport.

The show was launched by Fox Broadcasting in 1988, initially in seven major markets as a video twist on the post office most-wanted posters. The fledgling network selected as the host John Walsh, a photogenic, tough-talking father of a Florida boy who was kidnapped and murdered in 1981.

Walsh emerged as a national advocate for laws making it easier to track missing children and their abductors. The faces of the missing on milk cartons, as well as the National Center for Missing and Exploited Children, came about as the result of the lobbying and advocacy of the grief-stricken Walsh and his wife, Revé. The Florida couple's son, Adam, had been kidnapped in 1981 from a Sears department store in Hollywood, and his severed head was found two weeks later. The case remained unsolved until 2008, when authorities pinned it on serial killer Ottis Toole. By that time, John Walsh had turned *America's Most Wanted* into a blockbuster catch-a-bad-guy hit, led by his blustery disdain for all things criminal and his unquestioning support of law enforcement.

Even before its debut, the program had the cooperation of law enforcement agencies, from the Federal Bureau of Investigation down to the smallest municipal police force. The show's first victory came just four days after its February 7, 1988, debut, when the FBI apprehended one of its top ten most wanted in New York City after a viewer tip.

The show's format was uncomplicated and easy to understand—reenactments of crimes, dramatized for effect, with actors, complemented by photos of the actual

criminals and a phone number where viewers could call
in their tips.

Jon Leiberman was among the first of the crew to arrive in Indianapolis. An Emmy-winning correspondent
for *America's Most Wanted*, Leiberman's face was a
staple to the millions of *AMW* viewers, and his strident
anticrime vibe permeated every case he investigated and
every con he interviewed. The thirty-four-year-old reporter was seasoned with more than a decade of hard
news experience, and the Pender case was one more in a
series of high-profile crimes in his portfolio.

Leiberman was joined by producer Jenna Griffiths.
The two led a crime-stopping nomadic life that some
journalists dream of and others disdain. Theirs was a
world of hotels, airports, and rental cars, all navigated
while dealing with the lowest of society's life-forms and
hearing firsthand accounts of heartbreaking misdeeds.

Leiberman and Griffiths, along with a technical crew,
headed to the federal courthouse in downtown Indianapolis to meet with the cadre of law enforcement that was
searching for Sarah Pender. It was the mishmash of
agents, officers, and paper pushers that usually compose
most such bodies. The work generally falls on a couple
of hard workers, while the rest mix the fugitive search in
with their other duties. Although the case had been on
AMW's website since the day after Sarah's escape, it had
yielded little in the form of tips. Her picture, personal
stats, and crime were not getting the job done.

"It had become apparent that they needed our help,"

Leiberman says. "And I sensed a real urgency there. It was embarrassing to Corrections because an officer had helped her, and there was a fear that she had the capability to be violent."

Leiberman was verbally briefed on the case: the murder, the escape, the tips. He pored over a number of letters, pictures, and detritus found in the two boxes of personal items Sarah had sent to Jamie through the mail that were intercepted by Ryan Harmon. Then he headed up to Pendleton Correctional Facility. Rick Hull was waiting, and he wanted to talk to *America's Most Wanted*.

———

"If you have life to do in the penitentiary, it's everybody's dream to get out of the penitentiary one way or another—key word to that is *dream*," Rick Hull told Leiberman as tape rolled at the penitentiary. "Some people just don't put it into action. Or have the resources to do so."

Hull was the killer interview, the guy who gives such statements without a blink or a stutter. He looked directly at Leiberman, a straight-ahead, man-to-man look that had earned him respect over the years despite his obvious moral and ethical flaws.

Hull's hour of tape was boiled down to just over two minutes that would make it to broadcast. In the portion that didn't, Hull denied that he was manipulated in any way by Sarah during their relationship, particularly with regard to the murder.

"He also minimized Sarah's role in the [murder]," Leiberman says. "He was forthcoming. He looked me right in the eye."

Hull also came across to Leiberman as sympathetic to Sarah's flight, "But he never came out and said so."

The next day, the crew headed for the scene of the escape, where they were met with a willing cast of characters who, in a moment of embarrassing frankness, essentially walked Leiberman and the cameras through the escape.

His escort was Jerry Newlin, the rotund internal affairs investigator at Rockville. Newlin had been at Rockville for thirty-five years, from when it was a rather antiquated facility to its current state as a modern, if somewhat coddling, prison. He had moved from guard to counselor and up the ranks before moving to internal affairs in 2002. He knew the place inside and out. Now, he was willing to tell the world how to escape from it.

He showed a pathway that is "sort of a covered area as far as observation" and walked Leiberman down the sidewalk to a guardhouse.

"As we walk up here we have a security checkpoint," Newlin explained, pointing to a glass and steel enclosure about six by six feet in size. "She comes up to this guard post, turns to the left here and proceeds to go on through this inner security fence that we have right here."

"Was anybody in this guard gate?" Leiberman asks, pointing to the hut, which was empty.

"No, at that time of day the post itself is not manned," Newlin said.

The two walked through the gate, up to a waiting prison van set there to show viewers the location, and Newlin told of how Sarah's inside help, guard Scott Spitler, secured her under a seat in the van.

"As they went through the security procedures in here, again she was not detected at that point," Newlin said, as video captured a comprehensive examination of the van inside and out.

But he left out one key element to the escape: no such examination was done in Sarah's case. In fact, Spitler got out of the van and had a short conversation with the guard at the final checkpoint, aware that such conversation would likely ensure no sweep was done. It was some crafty spin put on a situation in which the wheels of security came off.

"A couple of things went through my mind on that visit," Leiberman says. "First, if you are in here for a double murder, these are very lax accommodations. You have bunk beds, a nice exercise room, big-screen TVs with video-game consoles."

Despite the obvious shortcomings in the prison's security, Leiberman says that the inside help Sarah had secured—a compromised and money-hungry Spitler— was the key to her freedom.

"If you have someone inside willing to help you, escape becomes much easier," he says. "A lot of mistakes were made that day. But without Scott Spitler, she does not get out."

The next day, more interviews with local law enforcement figures were done, including the camera-friendly prosecutor Larry Sells, Indianapolis Police captain Mark Rice, who was a lieutenant when he oversaw the investigation of the murders, and, finally, U.S. Marshals agent Ryan Harmon, the man chasing Sarah, who was so busy he barely had time to sit. He was now becoming obsessed with a quarry who, so far, had outwitted him.

The episode was edited over the next two weeks and was scheduled for a September 13 broadcast. Sarah by then would be sitting in the middle of the nation's second-largest city, making her detection ever more difficult.

———

Ryan Harmon was reluctant to spend his time on anything other than the pursuit of Sarah Pender.

When *AMW* came to town, he was unamused. Harmon was working the case—he had no time for cameras and the distraction of the camera.

"Have you got a second to talk?" Leiberman asked a reluctant Harmon as the crew set up for the briefing with law enforcement at the federal courthouse, a five-story edifice more than one hundred years old in the middle of downtown.

The meeting was being held several doors down from Harmon's office. The *AMW* correspondent had been told that Harmon was the primary hunter in the Pender case. His insight would be valuable to the episode. Sticking his head in to chat would set the tone, Leiberman thought.

"No, I really don't," Harmon said, preoccupied. *AMW* had already gone through the intercepted boxes of Sarah's personal effects that had been sitting on his desk.

Wasn't that enough? He had heard they wanted him to go on camera, but that would take time, and frankly, every second was making him itch with anticipation of a break in the case.

Leiberman's amicable manner never wavered.

"How about we just go get a Coke?" he offered. The vending machines down the hall would at least afford some walking time.

They chatted about the case, Leiberman leading and Harmon answering quickly. Tips? Yes, there were some, Harmon said. In fact, he was just getting ready to head to Pendleton to speak with Rick Hull.

That's funny, Leiberman said. So are we.

"I don't want to go on camera; I really just don't have time for this," Harmon said. "Good luck."

Leiberman persisted gently, allowing that time was indeed money.

"We are intertwined with the process of finding Pender," he explained. "This is as important to us as it is to you."

Harmon began to see that *AMW*'s presence was a blessing rather than a time-sucking curse. More tips. More chances. Millions of viewers.

"OK, let's do it," Harmon agreed, setting a time for the next day. The shoot took an hour.

———

Harmon's quest included twice-weekly visits to Rockville Correctional Facility, where inmates would hear something and want to help, hoping in the process to get some sort of juice that would trickle up and maybe, just maybe, garner favors inside the system or help when it came time to face a parole board.

"It would be after 9:30 at night that I would go out there," Harmon says. "I couldn't go in during the day because other inmates might see me, and the inmate didn't want to be seen talking to me; the other girls would know someone was snitching. So the prison would help me set up a ruse and get the tipster into a place we could talk."

Harmon would visit with anyone who wanted to talk, leaving him to discern who among them was trustworthy. Was it Jamie Long, one of the prime Pender accomplices and one who swore her fealty to Sarah? Was it Kimberly Stull, aka KP, Sarah's prison girlfriend who had helped her escape and was the proud holder of a "coochie coupon" from Sarah, entitling her to "any sexual favor she wants"? Maybe even Rick Hull, the man who waffled so many times on the blame for the original crime that no one could believe a word from his mouth?

"I had all these people working for me, and none of them knew I was working the other one," Harmon says. It was a throwback to the days when he worked cases on public corruption; he knew he was onto something only when stories from disparate sources started to line up.

He was also getting Crime Stoppers tips, many of which he would follow up on. Several times, Harmon and other agents knocked on doors in seedy Indianapolis neighborhoods. Sometimes they didn't knock.

"I was looking under every rock, every lead that came through those Crime Stoppers or from the prison system.

I did search warrants and false leads that came through the prison intelligence system. And I felt certain these were things that were close. Sometimes, we would blow the doors off a place on a tip."

When sleep came, it would sometimes be 4 a.m., Harmon climbing into bed beside his wife and thinking like a criminal, waiting for light to come so he could begin the chase again.

———

Setting such traps as Harmon did meant there were others doing his work. One of those was Anthony Kelly,* a close friend of Sarah's who was doing state time for murder, who agreed to help find Sarah after it was explained to him that Sarah could well die in a hail of bullets if and when she was finally discovered and she resisted. Kelly had befriended Sarah and her mother, Bonnie, over the years. Word was out that Sarah was not going to go back to prison, knowing full well that she would be placed in the most severe isolation humanly and legally possible as punishment for her escape. It was this possibility of Sarah's death by cop that convinced Kelly that he had to help, as repulsive as the notion was.

As he had done previously with a number of female inmates at Rockville, Harmon provided Kelly with a cell phone, with the agreement of the Department of Correction. Some of the first calls went to Bonnie Prosser, Sarah's mom, in Florida. It was a fairly sure thing that Sarah would try to reach out again, having touched base with her mother within the first forty-eight hours of her escape. Bonnie had become friends with Kelly over the years, occasionally visiting him, and now, both shared concern for Sarah's well-being. Kelly told Bonnie that all he wanted to do was help Sarah evade the cops.

Bonnie's primary concern was keeping her daughter safe and free—a mother's instinct that rarely falters.

Kelly primed Bonnie with a rumor that Sarah was being bounced around house-to-house through an underground network of ex-inmate lesbians, something that Harmon had picked up early on. Though untrue, it was something that Harmon latched onto for some time and that was quite feasible.

Kelly relayed this rumor to Bonnie, who was astounded, as she knew an escaped convict would always deliver a reward when caught.

"She knows now there's a bounty on her head," Bonnie said in one of the calls in early October. "Her own sister will turn her in. I can't believe that she is that stupid."

At the same time, Bonnie told Kelly the truth—that she had not heard from Sarah since that first call in the early stages of the breakout—but that she would like to put in motion the groundwork for obtaining a fake ID for Sarah.

In working Bonnie, Kelly pretended that he had gotten a call from Sarah and that she was safe.

"She told me she would get back in touch but she has to get settled in first," Kelly said to Bonnie. "I told her it could be six months. 'You have to make sure you're safe, that's number one.'"

He then talked about getting Sarah some kind of fake identification that would make it easier for her to assume a new life. Kelly claimed to have a contact that could get her a new driver's license.

"The papers, I can do that . . . this is coming from the [Department of Motor Vehicles], it is really legitimate. You can hand them to an officer and they are legit. This is not some little bullshit."

"How hard is it to get a birth certificate, does it come with that?" Bonnie asked.

"I'll work it out, I'll figure something out," Kelly said, adding that the certificate may be a counterfeit but it would be foolproof. Then the talk turned to money—a fake ID, with its attendant papers, can be pricey, running thousands on the black market. Kelly mentioned no price, but Bonnie was worried.

"It may be awhile before I can come up with it," she said, referring to the cost. "It's not an emergency right at this moment. It doesn't have to be tomorrow but I would like to have it just in case. What I'll do is figure out a name and a birth date."

"Figure out the info you want and I'll shoot it over to my people," Kelly promised.

It was one more trap Harmon was working, and God knows, he was trying everything.

———

Tom Welch drove with Sarah sitting peacefully beside him down U.S. Highway 30, his Cadillac CTS tilted toward Chicago. Sarah's destiny was out of her hands by now. As an escapee whose face was soon to be beamed across the nation to three million viewers of *AMW*, she had every right to be as paranoid as anyone. But instead, she continued to live her life as she pleased, with few thoughts given to hiding or trying to be someone else.

Sarah headed for the home of the niece of a friend of Welch's. Despite her compromised status, Sarah was still presented with options.

There was Welch's friend Bob, in Nolanville, Texas, south of Dallas, who had a catering truck that serviced construction sites. The work would be low level for Sarah, and it wasn't certain how long he could keep her employed. And sitting in Texas with a federal search on her head might not be the best option for Sarah. The state's law-and-order buzz made it a lousy place to disappear.

But there was another option. Bob's niece Angel lived in Chicago's South Side and worked at a printing shop that was fielding a glut of business for the presidential campaign of Illinois senator Barack Obama. The work was simple—cut, fold, and stuff envelopes, a task that presented the campaign with ready-made mailers.

"She can come up there and stuff envelopes for Obama because they are going to be sending out flyers and stuff," Bob told Welch, who by now was enveloped in a love-hate deal with Sarah—he loved the sex, and he hated the ferrying about of his human cargo.

The story of Sarah's identity was different as presented to Bob and Angel, though; rather than Ashley Thompson, the girl who was fleeing her abusive, estranged husband,

Sarah was now Ashley Thompson, Welch's niece, feasible given the two-decade age difference. It made things more conducive to caretaking.

"So I called Bob and Bob called his niece Angel," Welch said. "I took [Sarah], dropped her off, and I left."

Angel lived not far from U.S. Cellular Field, in an area that can best be described as ghetto on the upswing. The area, abutting the Hyde Park neighborhood, is a mix of tough urban and collegiate and is home to the University of Chicago and the Museum of Science and Industry. Students and up-and-coming professionals still lived there because of its reasonable rents and proximity to mass transit, and Sarah could swing her look to grad student or fledgling yuppie with no trouble.

Still, it was not a place Welch wanted for Sarah, but the work provided cover for her. He had no better plan. And she was three short hours away by car.

By the following weekend, Welch was back, picking up Sarah from her shared quarters on the bad side of town and ferrying her away to a Best Western in Merrillville, Indiana, where the two could again cavort, hitting the Horseshoe Casino in nearby Hammond, Indiana.

The season was changing, even in this second week of September, something Sarah could not have planned for in her wardrobe. Each day was a gift, of course, and catching a chill was the least of her concerns. But Welch, in the flush of love, could only want to help.

"We went to Walmart in Merrillville . . . and the Gander Mountain thing because it was getting cold," Welch said. Gander Mountain was one more chain store aimed at the outdoor crowd, filled with down vests, hunting gear, and weapons of all varieties. Welch bought Sarah some jeans and a sweater at Walmart and some other items at Gander.

Sarah had managed to score a better job in the week on her own in Chicago. Through Angel—a convoluted connection scheme via Angel's best friend's brother and his father—Sarah landed work with a construction company that was looking for some help north of the city. The Sciortino Group in Cicero needed help with some estimating and blueprint reading. In an interview with several of the bosses there, Sarah, as Ashley Thompson, told her sad story once again. "It was the cop-husband story and how I didn't want to be found," Sarah says. "I was living with Angel still, and they paid me in cash."

Her commute to work was an hour-plus grind, and dangerous to boot, up from Hyde Park either via the number 6 bus or the Pink Line of the El. Her occasional bouts of paranoia were nothing compared to the relative danger in the quickly shortening days.

Welch had bought her a Swiss Army knife and a canister of mace at Gander Mountain. She needed some self-defense, he felt.

"She was going from the South Side, she was going from the bus station down in the south part of the Loop, which is not a good area . . . then going up north," Welch said.

Their weekends were still spent together, with Tom driving into the city, picking Sarah up.

Sarah used a new laptop computer Welch bought her for her Sciortino work, messing with blueprints and CAD drawings for projects. With the computer, Sarah could do much of her work out of her home, or wherever she was at the time. Her e-mail address was ashtom0808@ yahoo.com, a tweak to the month and year of her liberation. Her password was haveaniceday.

By the time Welch returned to Chicago for another rendezvous two weeks later, Sarah had moved closer to her work, again, working her magic. She told the folks at the family-run Sciortino Group that the commute from the South Side was taking up four hours of her day. Even with her occasional virtual office, a part-time commute was onerous. She told them she would like an apartment closer to work and that because of the requisite background check, she could not rent one herself in case her cop husband had traces out on her.

"So they said they would get the apartment in the company's name," Sarah said. She forged a deal under which she was paid $350 a week in cash for her work, plus $500 a month toward the $800 monthly rent on her small apartment, number 3-E, at 2204 West Farwell Avenue in Rogers Park. The neighborhood was trendy old-school, with brick apartment buildings that still had steam heat and the original wood floors. Her utilities were also under the name of the company and paid for.

Sarah figured it worked out to about $20 an hour she was making. She even got cable TV in her own assumed name; no Social Security number was required for that service.

Her new commute to the job site was easier and allowed her to simply live like a regular person, with little concern over who might identify her. It was a big city. She would walk six blocks to Touhy Avenue and grab the 97 bus to the site in Skokie. The line was filled with commuters reading the morning *Trib* or worrying about day-to-day life. It was a stretch to think that one of them might catch a convicted murderer squished into the narrow bench seats or hanging on the chrome pole.

Sarah was making some cash. Her expenses were minimal, and the $350 a week was more than enough to keep her fed. It was enough to make her consider another move.

"There were times that I had $1,500 in my pocket and I actually thought about getting on a bus and visiting my dad in Seattle or going to Florida to see my mom," Sarah said. "Or even going to New York and getting lost. But I wanted to stay with Tom. Things were going too well to leave."

Welch was doing his part for sure.

He got Sarah a cell phone on his private business account. His visits were faithful, and he indulged her with fine dinners, and she gorged herself on margaritas.

"She really loved those margaritas," Welch said.

Meanwhile, in addition to lining up a cadre of law-breaking helpers—cons, ex-cons, and street people—Ryan Harmon was playing hunches and taking chances. One of the latter was a visit to Sarah's father, Roland Pender.

Harmon boarded a plane and headed for Bellevue, Washington, to a condominium on a street lined with tall pines in a home built on a hillside affording a view of a shallow valley filled with more pine trees and rooftops.

Roland had done well for himself in the Pacific Northwest.

He was preparing to leave on a trip to Florida to see his daughter Jennifer. Harmon knew this already because he had been reading Roland's e-mails, secured via a court order. And, being a diligent detective, Harmon also knew quite a few other things about Roland as well as his wife, Wendy.

She was a librarian from the Midwest. The two had met online. Roland courted her from Bellevue, and they first met when he was in Indiana to visit Sarah in prison. She was once-divorced with no children and was a person of faith. Harmon figured it would be good to get in her good graces right away. She was Roland's light, he calculated, and his voice of reason. And that's what Ryan Harmon was here to appeal to.

The hour Harmon chose to arrive—a still-dark 6 a.m.—surprised both Roland and Wendy, although Wendy rose early most days.

Roland was rubbing his eyes after being awoken, walking into the living room to find Ryan Harmon sitting there. Pender crossed his arms. He was not going to open up.

"You know, neither of us can control the conviction right now," Harmon said, after some brief cordialities on his part. "I flew out here to let you know that this is not all about hunting down your daughter and putting a bullet into her and 'game over.' I plan to go my whole career without ever firing my weapon."

Roland Pender stared.

"If she went out in a blaze of glory and they killed her and you had the opportunity to keep that from happening, could you live with that?" Harmon asked.

"I don't know," Pender said. He was coming around.

"You would have the bloodstained hands," Harmon said.

The two looked at each other. The tension ebbed some, and they talked. About other things. About living in the beautiful Northwest. About travel. About anything other than the reason a federal agent was sitting in the living room trying to capture an escaped convict who happened to be the daughter of this rather gentle-looking man, of average height, with a face framed by a reddish beard and tousled reddish hair.

Two hours later, Harmon rose to leave.

"What are your plans coming up here?" Harmon asked as he walked toward the door. Roland could easily have said nothing, or lied, or simply told him it was none of his business.

"I'm going to visit Jennifer in Florida," Roland said.

It was then that Harmon knew that if Sarah were to

reach out to her father, chances were good that he would get a call from Roland.

"He understood that Sarah being killed was a lot worse than her being in prison," Harmon says.

And now, he had one more person in his camp that would like to see Sarah back behind bars.

CHAPTER 9

The first episode of *America's Most Wanted* detailing Sarah's escape aired on September 13, 2008. Her breakout led the broadcast with an eight-minute segment that was classic *AMW*, featuring a bevy of information, interviews, and graphics that only insiders like Leiberman and his crew could obtain, including prison photos, some with a visiting Jamie Long, and video of Sarah strumming an acoustic guitar and singing for inmates at the Rockville Correctional Facility.

Host John Walsh introduced the piece by calling Pender an "artist."

"Our first story tonight is about an artist," Walsh said, holding his hands up and using his index and middle fingers to emulate quotation marks. It was trademark Walsh, a bit of snarky hostility from the get-go.

"Some artists can take a block of clay and mold it and

manipulate it into anything they can think of," Walsh continued. "But the artist on our first story is a con artist. She manipulates people instead of clay. And even when she was sent off to prison, she never stopped working her craft. . . . Everyone around her was putty in her hands."

Then correspondent Jon Leiberman took over, noting that Sarah was among the seventy prisoners at Rockville serving a life sentence, narrating over a thudding beat and angular camera shots of steel cages and industrial staircases.

Viewers first saw Sarah as a long-haired, hippie-esque girl hitting a down strum on an acoustic guitar. In another context, Sarah would have looked like a coffeehouse maven.

"As far as an inmate, you could look at her and say she was a model inmate," Jerry Newlin, internal affairs investigator at Rockville, told Leiberman. "She was a pleasant person to be around. She has been a volunteer in a lot of recreational activities to support the inter-action and the community inside the prison."

"If people needed help with legal matters, she was there to help them review their case or to get forms they needed so they could file motions and different things," added John Poer, another prison administrator. "She helped people with their taxes."

"She was a helper," Poer concluded with a smile.

Cut to Larry Sells, who prosecuted Sarah and deemed her in his segment a "very, very dangerous criminal."

"She has a Charles Manson–like ability to manipulate people," Sells said, his brow grim as he sat at a desk looking up from a pile of transcripts and murder-scene photos from the case file. By 2008, Sells was retired, but he still bore the hard-boiled manner that had cut such a fearsome figure in his younger days.

And then, a surprise: Richard Hull is shown, his head still shaved, the same facial hair framing the middle of his face in a Fu Manchu style. He is still enormous, dwarfing the guard who pushes a door open for him as Hull enters the interview room with his hands cuffed in front of him.

"It's just part of the drug game," Hull began, his eyes drooping, speaking about his fate of incarceration. He looked sad, resigned, defeated. "I mean they say at least the two places, the penitentiary or the morgue. Hence, here I am."

The screen then cut to a brief reenactment of the 2000 murders that landed Sarah and Hull in prison—done with actors much more attractive and clean-cut than the real players.

"Drew and I were into the meth business," Hull narrated. "We ran a lot of meth. He said, uh, the hell with me, the hell with my money and if I didn't like it, he was gonna blow my mom's house up."

The actors playing Hull and Andrew Cataldi, the male victim, get into a fight, with Cataldi challenging Hull: "What are you going to do about it?"

The actor playing Hull looked to Sarah's portrayer, who nodded assent, as if urging him to act on some pre-arranged order.

"I grabbed a gun right then and there and I shot him

and his girlfriend," Hull told Leiberman. In future *AMW* episodes, the comment, delivered without a hint of emotion, would be replayed, its evil subtlety playing into the overall vibe of the presentation.

But the desired message was the same at all times.

"Hull pulled the trigger because Pender told him to," Leiberman asserted in the narrative.

Then Larry Sells came back on: "She has the ability to seduce others to commit atrocious acts. The evidence was overwhelming that if she didn't pull the trigger, she did everything else."

A jump cut back to Hull was revealing, as he asserted that he knew of Sarah's escape plans as well as her flirting with Scott Spitler, the guard who let Sarah run. In fact, Hull said, he and Sarah had been in "constant" contact through contraband cell phones.

"She told me she was having, you know, a business relationship with somebody there," Hull said. He said Sarah described Spitler as "middle aged, you know . . . She told me 'Man, he's acting like he's going through a midlife crisis or something like that.'"

Leiberman then walked viewers through the escape, complete with wardrobe switch and a walk down the very hallway and sidewalk Sarah escaped through.

Next Leiberman sat down with Ryan Harmon, who explained that "Sarah's a convicted murderer, she's a con. She did con some cons to help her. But since she's been out, she's told these people [referring to Spitler and Jamie Long], 'You knew what you were doing when you were helping me.' These people that are in jail right now.

She's flushed them down the toilet like she flushed two bodies in a Dumpster."

Leiberman even got an inmate to comment, without showing her face. The unnamed inmate, around forty years old, was pulling clothes from a washing machine inside the prison.

"Is this gonna be on a most wanted thing?" she asks, her back to the camera. Yes, she is told.

"I don't think they'll get her . . . she had too much inside help," the woman said.

The segment ended with Leiberman correctly asserting that "Pender is like a chameleon," while a montage of photos of Sarah with varying hair styles and colors flooded the screen. "As you can see she has many different looks and could have changed her appearance by cutting and dyeing her hair. She's an Internet junkie. We know she's manipulative. And she's probably already working her charms on someone new."

———

As Hull described his role in the shootings, Willard Plank, who heads internal affairs for the Indiana Department of Correction, sat off camera and watched. Just before the taping began, Hull looked at Plank and promised, "If she's gonna get hold of me, she will get hold of me after this interview."

Coaching inmates to say something that might lure an escapee, or at least provide impetus for tips, is common in these settings. But Plank did not say anything and had no idea what was coming. When Hull uttered those chilling words, "I grabbed a gun right then and there and I shot him and his girlfriend," it was convincing. There was more to the statement, details, which would be used in future episodes as the chase for Sarah became more urgent.

And Hull would later regret helping.

"I said that stuff about me doing it on purpose," Hull says. "It was an enticement for her to come out of the woodwork. At that point, I had no hope for any relief in my sentence. But people who have known me my whole life saw that, people who had been in my corner and believed in me saw that. It wasn't true, and I looked like a complete jackass in front of them."

———

In keeping with John Walsh's "charmed" statement, well, Tom Welch was already charmed to the bottom of his heart. Some early October evenings, Sarah would be done with work and call him on his cell phone, via the cell phone he had specially gotten her on an account in the name of his trucking company, GC3 Logistics. Her salacious messages would cater to his sexual proclivity for oral sex, and the videos of Sarah masturbating, also sent via phone, were her own way of ensuring Welch kept her in mind at all times.

She would do this from her small apartment in the Rogers Park neighborhood of Chicago, a storied enclave in which former first lady Betty Ford was raised.

The dwelling, with wooden floors, a cramped bed-room with a mattress on the floor, and a flat-screen TV in the living area, was furnished with rented items provided by Welch. A sectional couch, a dining-room table and chairs, and a dresser were all part of this private world of Sarah's. The utilities—gas and electric—were provided by her employer, the Sciortino Group, which had agreed to sign for the apartment believing that Sarah was on the run from a crazed, abusive, estranged spouse.

In between the longing phone calls and sex messages, there were the visits from Welch, and sometimes, trips to nearby casinos and hotels.

The two would go out for dinner, like any other couple, on his visits to the Rogers Park apartment. Jesse's Mexican Grill on Western Avenue, a two-block walk through the fallen yellow leaves, was a favorite.

Sarah would order tiramisu; both would drink plenty.

It was a courtship, plain and simple. The escaped convict and the benevolent entrepreneur talked of love and murder. All in the open, even after the initial *America's Most Wanted* segment, and another shorter follow-up on September 27. Neither of them had seen the episodes, but they were aware they had aired. And it made no difference.

"It's not like she was in a motorcycle gang and was staying underground or whatever they do," Welch said. "We're not hiding anywhere. We're dating. We're dating. It's not like, there's a frickin' cop. There was none of that."

The September 27 *America's Most Wanted* update on Sarah hinted at a number of new tips, none of them solid.

The three-minute story led off a segment of the show called "All Points Bulletin," which focuses on criminals who are proving harder to catch than others. Host John Walsh called her a "cold-blooded killer who manipulated her way out of an Indiana prison."

Larry Sells again offered an ominous portrayal of Sarah: "She appears to be, on the surface, a sweet, fairly innocent and, even to a certain extent, helpless young lady. But lurking within is a dark, evil demon."

Ryan Harmon was convinced that Sarah was watching, and he directed a message at her: "Sarah Pender needs to know that there's no cave, no woods, no rock she can hide under. We're gonna find you Sarah."

Walsh told viewers again that Sarah was an "Internet junkie. She uses the screen names violet and ladybug." He said that cops had also received tips that had her headed for Florida or Connecticut and using the aliases Heather or Jennifer Davis. Walsh also said there was information coming in that Sarah might be taking care of an elderly man in eastern Indiana.

"There was a steady flow of tips from the time of the first episode," says *AMW*'s Leiberman. "None of them panned out."

One of the most promising tips sent the crew to a house on the south side of Indianapolis in October, when *AMW* returned to the city to film one more update shortly after the September 27 episode.

Harmon received some credible information on the street that Sarah was at a ramshackle house that was now home to Erin Rose, one of Sarah's inmate friends who had recently been released after serving a sentence for theft. Part of that came from some computer-server surveillance that saw messages at the home going from someone believed to be Sarah to Rose's father.

Warrant in hand, Harmon and a SWAT team, in standard bulletproof gear and with weapons drawn, descended on the home in the early morning.

"The game's over. She's got 110 years over her head, you don't," Harmon barked at the shirtless man who answered the door. "It's a matter of time. We're here for a reason."

But a search found nothing. The reality was that Sarah had never been there. Rose had logged on as Sarah, sending out a false message and giving Harmon some misplaced hope.

Harmon's desperation was palpable, and he was now becoming reluctant to even spend time on anything other than this chase. The next week Harmon spent in a topless joint called Patty's Showclub, a ten-minute drive from Club Venus, where Sarah had originally connected with Tom Welch and paved her way to a somewhat unfettered freedom.

It was a Crime Stoppers tip that led him to the place. A dancer had a tattoo on her ass similar to the bull's-eye Sarah sported. Red hair. Chunky.

"I spent four nights there because there was supposed to be a dancer who might be Sarah," Harmon says. "I spent a lot of money there. They thought I was a contractor in town temporarily."

The girl didn't show up for work for the first three

nights, and Harmon spent those evenings chatting up the girls, trying to find out when his girl would be in and what shift she would be working. On the fourth night, she showed up.

Wrong tattoo. This girl had an arrow, not a bull's-eye.

———————

On October 20, Sarah was placed on the U.S. Marshals' 15 Most Wanted fugitive list. The move was announced in a press release and touted a $25,000 reward for information leading to her capture.

A poster featured two inmate photos of Sarah, one from her prison ID and the other in her graduation cap from commencement day at the prison several years earlier, when she had matriculated with a business degree.

It stated her size at five feet eight and 150 pounds, with a butterfly tattoo on her left breast and a blue and red bull's-eye on her right buttock.

The list, which has been issued for the last twenty-five years, has resulted in two hundred fugitive arrests. Pender's appearance marks her as one of the few females to ever make it. And her listing was never determined to play a role in her fate.

"Sarah Pender is a dangerous fugitive and poses a threat to anyone she comes in contact with," Director John F. Clark of the U.S. Marshals Service said in a canned quote for the release. "Pender's addition as a 15 Most Wanted fugitive underscores our commitment to use all of our available resources to bring her to justice."

The release barely made it through the presidential

campaign chatter. One television news outlet in Indianapolis didn't even run anything until mid-November,
after the election. Sarah's flight was hardly breaking
through the news clutter, even locally. It was one more
thing in her favor. She couldn't have planned it better.

———————

The most wanted woman in America was cheered by the
election of Barack Obama as president of the United
States. Sarah had espoused her liberal views most of her
adult life, and Obama represented to her, as to much of
America, a breakthrough in society.

On November 4, tens of thousands of people turned
out to Grant Park, an hour train ride to Sarah's south in
downtown Chicago, to hear Illinois senator and president-
elect Obama deliver his acceptance speech. Sarah pondered the notion of being part of that throng, an escapee
from the justice system that the president would vow to
protect as commander in chief. She didn't see the irony
there, instead filtering it through the prism of herself as a
normal citizen.

"I wanted to experience it, but I was thinking, 'You
know, with all the police and stuff it's probably a really
dumb idea.' Although they wouldn't be looking for me,
it would be my luck. So I watched it on TV, recorded it
on my DVR."

Her digital video recorder had become familiar to her.
Although she was at first flummoxed by all of the choices
she had to make in just living daily life, Sarah had
quickly acclimated to using DVRs, flat-screen TVs, and

new laptop computers. Her life behind bars had arrested her technological development in some ways, of course. Windows Vista was easy for her to learn, and the emerging social networking held great allure for her, although she kept herself from indulging.

"I didn't e-mail anyone because I knew all that stuff they could trace real easy," Sarah said. She visited the *America's Most Wanted* site once. "I wouldn't check it a lot because if anybody goes, like they could check my name, so I would check on other people's stuff and then mine also."

Which meant she would see the comments posted on articles regarding her escape. Many former inmates would post comments, likely aware that Sarah was staying at least somewhat connected.

On August 11, a week after Sarah's breakout, commentators hit the story of her escape on the website of the NBC affiliate in Indianapolis.

"i was at r-ville for 4 yrs and the headcount is weird but i dont believe sara should have been treated any different then others she may have killed someone but they were convicted felons too," posted tara. "sara was a good person that doesnt have anything to loose shes there for life anyway."

And the trail continued at the Weekly Vice, a site devoted to aberrant crimes and criminals, where someone using the handle "anonymous" simply posted "Run, Sarah Jo Pender, Run!" That was followed up with some advice:

"RUN, SARAH RUN! Just get into some place and lay low for about 5 years. Trust no one. Go nowhere.

Then get your ass to some safe country and live your life. No one should have to pay a lifetime for the dubious mistakes made in their 20's. My prayers are with you girl. I surround you with compassion. Kb."

At Brokencontrollers.com, a poster by the handle of whatalife40 on August 14 wrote, "I knew Sarah for about a month and a half back in 2000..we spend time together in marion co. jail. if someone were to pull this off and get away with it, it would be sarah. She is smart but knows how to get people to think she is something great and sly in a way. Good luck out there and I hope you make it on the run always!!!!! Lm."

It was whatalife40's first and only post at the site. But the most active discussion by far was taking place at a site called People You'll See in Hell, or pysih.com. Several girls claiming to know Sarah or to have spent time in Rockville posted, some pro-Sarah and some not so favorable.

Someone with the identity spam_turkeybologna wrote on October 19, "I was released from Rockville a few months prior to Sarah escape. I actually knew her well. She thought that the world revolved around her and was God's gift to earth. Spitler was actually a really cool guy and I feel kinda bad for him because I believe that Sarah had him totally brainwashed. . . . That girl is nuts!"

Another, more charitable participant, giving herself the name of an ex-Rockville inmate, Cassidy Burgess, wrote on October 5, "I am a ex offender at Rockville. Sarah Pender is not a monster. She did not kill anyone, nor intended to have them killed. She wil not kill anyone. I believe the girl deserved her freedom. She got a raw deal. I know her personally and I think its great shes free. Shes a beautiful person and so intelligent. She was like a caged animal and now shes got her freedom. So the rest of you talk shit if you want, but shes not going to hell."

The anonymity of the Internet no doubt loosened tongues and gave a platform to any fake who wanted it. But there was no doubt, it was a world in which Webbies everywhere were lingering, watching, and even participating.

———

The November 15 episode of *America's Most Wanted* devoted nine minutes to Sarah. Clearly, her ability to escape detection had everyone flummoxed, from the seasoned manhunt agent Harmon to the persistent Walsh.

This time, the show began with Walsh walking amid confusing props, such as a glittering neon dollar sign and a billboard reading "Tropicana Mobil Park."

"Tonight we're hosting some of the most incredible magic acts in the world, really skilled illusionists, specializing in eye-popping deception and head-scratching escapes," Walsh said. "Well, for the last few weeks, we've been chasing down a bad girl who's also proven to be a master of deception, a skill cops say helped her escape from prison."

Walsh was generous with his praise for Sarah's ability to remain free. But it also indicated a frustration among law enforcement.

The body of the nine-minute segment began abruptly,

with a reprise of the dramatized murder and Richard Hull giving the chilling play-by-play in his matter-of-fact delivery.

This time, Hull gave a chilling account of the murders, complete with demonic stares and a stoic narration.

"I grabbed the shotgun, I didn't you know, aim it, point it or nothin' like that, I fired it from the waist and I, uh, shot him in the throat area killin' him pretty much instantly. Trish was sitting on the couch."

"Then what did you do?" Leiberman asked.

"I pulled the trigger."

"One shot into her?"

"Twice. As soon as I shot him, I just pointed at her and it just glanced off the side of her. Then I shot her in the back of the head. These two homicides they were not planned. If they were planned I probably wouldn't have shot them with a 12-gauge deer slug. Leaves a nasty mess."

Leiberman then asserts that police believe that Sarah was the "mastermind of the massacre."

The highlight of the episode, though, was the interview Leiberman landed with Jamie Long, who had previously refused to speak with *AMW*.

"She's a very beautiful girl," Long said, starting the interview benignly. "She's got a great personality."

"Was she your friend, was she your lover, was she your confidant?" Leiberman asked.

"She was my wife," Long said plainly, looking straight at her interviewer, almost defiantly.

The narrative spoke of Sarah and her relationship

with Spitler, and Long had told Leiberman, off camera, that Sarah called Spitler "her bulldog."

On camera, Long said that Sarah had told her that Spitler was "on board. . . . He was gonna do whatever it took to help her."

"Do you believe that she manipulated Spitler?" Leiberman asked.

"She's a woman," Long replied, with a twisted little smile. "Absolutely. Pussy does make the world go 'round."

Then, Long cackled, a self-assured, almost taunting verbal scorn.

The word *pussy* was bleeped for broadcast, of course. But everyone knew what she said.

More narration and footage followed, then there was more camera time for Long.

Leiberman asked her about the moment Sarah appeared at her car door in the prison parking lot.

"When she got in your car, was there a feeling of disbelief, that wow this—" Leiberman asked.

"Well yeah," Long said, cutting him off. Then with belligerent sarcasm she posed, "Ya think?" as if the question were the dumbest ever posed.

"I can't believe she's sitting next to me in this vehicle and we're driving away."

It was a difficult interview to watch. Perhaps just as difficult to conduct.

"I spoke with her the better part of an hour," Leiberman says. "She was very combative and not apologetic at all. I asked her if she would do it again and she said,

'Not exactly the same way.' She did not seem sympathetic to catching Sarah at all."

The piece ended with a rallying call for Sarah, which was, curiously, the same as that used for a conservative politician, Sarah Palin, who had been part of the defeated presidential ticket just two weeks prior.

Long told of letting Sarah off in Indianapolis, telling her to not look back. Then, a cut to a grinning Long, again the cackle, and the money shot: "Run, Sarah, run."

Harmon, who was off camera and present for the interview, beamed. He hoped Long's rallying cry would elicit Sarah or one of her friends to get enthused about the cops' inability to find her and slip up—maybe a loose comment to a friend or a giddy call from Sarah to one of her parents, a call that could be traced to her location.

The segment ended with some vastly erroneous information: Pender confidants claiming that Sarah was selling sex for cocaine "and will do anything to get a fix."

The notion that Sarah would be stupid enough to get involved in such a low-level activity speaks to the growing desperation that law enforcement was feeling. Sarah had never had an addiction problem at all, and the false tips were obviously aimed at throwing Sarah's pursuers off the trail. The cops had been played, plain and simple. To entertain the drug angle was naive and grasping.

"There was concern that she might be getting farther away," says Leiberman. "I don't think there was a sense that she was going to be gone forever. There was never a sense that she was in the wind. But there was some worry that was growing."

Tips were now coming in that had Sarah being sighted in every Walmart in the land, from Florida to Oregon. The clues were baseless—how many girls could fit Sarah's basic description?—but many of them were checked out. Then there were the wannabe sleuths.

A Sarasota, Florida–based private investigator named Bill Warner, situated just south of where Sarah's mother, Bonnie, lived, posted a press release on the Internet on November 15. It quoted a federal spokesman, accurately, but it unnecessarily inflated Florida's location as a place to be examined.

"Since her escape from prison, we've had information that she's in Florida and we believe she may still be here in the Tampa-Bradenton area," read the release, its origin a website run by a retired firefighter. The release quoted Dan Winfield, a spokesman from the U.S. Marshals Service in Orlando. Winfield was a U.S. Marshal deputy based in the department's Orlando office. The release went on to say, "Authorities request that Anna Maria Island residents (Bradenton) be on the lookout for Sarah Jo Pender, 29, who escaped from Rockville Correctional Facility in Indiana on Aug. 4 and may attempt to reach relatives who are Anna Maria Island residents. A $25,000 reward is offered for information leading directly to her arrest. If you have information about Sarah Pender's whereabouts, immediately contact your nearest U.S. Marshals' office or call the Marshals' 24-hour hotline at 1-800-336-0102. Sources say that Sarah loved her long blond, curly hair, but since she has been out of prison, police have heard reports that she might have cut it off and dyed it black or brown. Could be working the strip joints for cash and men, she plays off of men for shelter and access to vehicles and the internet, has used her cell phone (a throwaway) to text old jail 'gal pals' in the last two weeks along with e-mails."

Tom Welch and Sarah took in the November 15 *AMW* episode from a king bed at the Knight's Inn in Lafayette, Indiana. The budget motel sat off Interstate 65 between Chicago and Indianapolis, and it was one more in a string of small motels that Sarah and Tom would shack up in sometimes, even though Sarah's Chicago apartment afforded them the privacy an illicit relationship— not to mention the harboring of a fugitive—required.

That evening was the first time they had actually been sitting around with the TV on and something regarding Sarah came on. Most of the *AMW* account was accurate, Sarah says, "because by the second showing they really focused on how I got out of prison."

Welch was taken aback, even as Sarah pointed out her version of the truth and how *AMW* had distorted it.

"I cannot believe I am doing this," Welch told her. "I must be insane."

He had wanted to know everything about the crime and the escape from the start. But this was more than he was ready to take.

"That's when I started going, 'Holy shit,'" Welch said. "I'm sitting here and I don't know what to do. I honestly don't know what to do. They keep saying you call in anonymously, but how can you call in anonymously? If I call you, it can't be anonymous. OK? I'm sitting there, I don't know what to do. This is when it hit me, that I don't know what I got myself into. When I saw the reenactment, when I saw, even though there wasn't any blood, it hit me. That's when I started, how do I get out? How do I get out of this thing?"

So he said exactly what came into his mind: Welch turned to her and cuddled her under his arm.

"Why don't you turn yourself in?" he asked. "Is it really worth all this?"

Sarah had already been thinking of the future, talking about the upcoming Thanksgiving holiday and the loneliness incumbent on her with her fugitive status. She was not going to be able to see her relatives, and Welch would be with his own wife and family for the holiday. She was not happy about the coming days. She loved Christmas, the music especially. One of her favorites was "Christmas Cookies," by George Strait, but she also loved the traditional carols. It was a season she had adored when she was free.

When they began talking again, Welch for the first time pondered his legal risk as well as the possibility of helping Sarah through the system rather than around it. But he was trying to grasp a world that was foreign to him, one of journalism and think tanks and causes that worked to prove innocence.

"What if we got Geraldo?" Welch asked, referring to the talk-show host Geraldo Rivera, whose show was coincidentally also broadcast by the Fox News Channel, operated by the same company, News Corporation, as *AMW*'s broadcast.

"Because I have seen Geraldo do some shit, you know? The guy takes a risk. Maybe we could get Geraldo to get with you, and he's got enough clout to where if you are truly wanting to get a new trial."

Sarah considered, silently. Rivera was known as a crusading talk-show host who uses the news industry as a platform. His animated 1988 interview with—again, coincidence—Charles Manson remains the stuff of legend, with Rivera calling Manson a "mass murdering dog." Maybe this was an approach that would work. Sarah had maintained since the crime that she was unfairly sentenced, and maybe a crusader like Rivera would see that.

"I would probably do that," Sarah said.

The words were lost quickly, however. No matter what, she was almost certain Welch would not roll on her. He was now on the hook, culpable for keeping her free and on the lam. The two didn't talk much about Geraldo again.

CHAPTER 10

One of the first items of business among most people on the lam is procuring some form of false identification. Successful execution of this task has allowed a number of prison escapees to live freely and undetected for years. Some are eventually caught, such as drug offender Susan LeFevre, a California mother of three who was arrested in 2008 after thirty-two years of freedom. Her freedom was spent without much of a hitch, and she had even worked. She had appropriated another person's Social Security number.

For Sarah Pender, coming up with a fictitious name and birth date was smart. She gave herself a fake Social Security number, in case it was needed, changing only one digit at the end of her nine-number identity.

Although Sarah was undoubtedly street-smart and knew her way around the criminal community, her pursuit of a false ID was misplaced. She mistakenly felt she would have to enter the drug world to secure an ID when, actually, she was living in the middle of ground zero for false identification.

Federal agents had for years made arrests in connections with fake ID documentation organizations around Chicago. The southwest part of the city, especially, was known as a hotbed of illegal identification for newly arrived illegal immigrants seeking a clean ID for getting a job.

Sarah, though, felt that hitting the streets and making connections was how it would have to be done, if she were to do it at all. She was unaware that Social Security cards, fake green cards, and fake driver's licenses could be had for $500 and up at some storefronts. No doubt a man with Tom Welch's means would have been able to provide the capital to score a very good ID, perhaps even that of a deceased person, which is the gold mine in the false ID underworld.

"Tom and I talked about that . . . in order to get an ID I was going to have to do some things," Sarah said. "I have to make some contacts. But I thought about it and I thought, 'I don't want to. I don't want to do drugs and I don't want to be around people who do drugs and who steal.'"

And she found that not having a government identification didn't pose any real troubles for her anyway: "You'd be amazed at how much you can achieve without ID."

So she simply remained Ashley for the time being, content to work at the Sciortino Group, working first out of the central office on West Addison in north Chicago, then at a warehouse office on the site of a demolition project further north near Skokie.

Her most determined attempt at getting away from being Sarah was getting rejuvenator injections in her lips to make her mouth wider and plumper, more voluptuous. A more glamorous look was appropriate for the circles in which she might be traveling, a professional world that would embrace her computer-assisted drawing skills and her organizational acumen as well as her looks.

But first, Sarah would take some time off from work in November to straighten things out with the fictitious husband of Ashley Thompson. At least that's what she told her employer around the middle of the month. Instead, she headed for Indiana for a string of budget motels and motor inns that had become her refuge when she wanted to be near Tom Welch, her married paramour. The Super 8 in Lebanon, Indiana, was one, then another joint in Lafayette. She was kept. But soon she would prepare to make another move.

——————

As Sarah slept away in Indiana over the Thanksgiving holiday, there was at least the appearance of hope for her return to the dinner table at her mother's place in Bradenton, Florida. At least that's how it appeared to Lauren Miniaci, who was now tied to the family through a custody dispute over Samantha, a ten-year-old girl born to Sarah's sister, Jennifer, and Lauren's current husband, Randy, in 1998, before Randy and Jennifer split in 2001.

Lauren and Randy married in 2004, and because of Samantha, the couple was in fairly constant contact with Jennifer, although not on friendly terms.

"The family was acting strange just before Thanksgiving," Lauren says. "There was some thought that Sarah was coming down here. The family was kind of rounding everyone up to come over."

Jennifer usually played down her own interest in Sarah's fate, although she had at times expressed dismay over the entire situation.

"My sister thinks she is going to get out and she never is," she told Lauren one day.

Bonnie Prosser, Sarah's mother, wouldn't talk about much of anything with Lauren.

But nonetheless, Lauren noticed a little more animated chatter about the possibilities of the holiday. A sense of cheer, if you will.

"We wondered what they knew," she says.

———

Tips had dwindled, even in the wake of the November 15 episode of *America's Most Wanted*. It was extremely rare for the crime show to run four episodes on a single fugitive in three months, but Sarah was proving to be a rare criminal. She was joining an upper echelon of hyperintelligent, on-the-run murderers, and in the process, making the pursuit a joke. Sarah was in some esteemed criminal-underworld company when it came to staying free and on the lam.

Spree murderer and serial killer Ted Bundy escaped from the Garfield County Jail in Glenwood Springs, Colorado, in December 1977 and eluded law enforcement for forty-six days, running to Tallahassee, Florida, and killing three more victims before being arrested.

Richard Lee McNair was a career criminal serving three life sentences for murder when he broke out of a maximum-security lockup in Pollock, Louisiana, in April 2006. He was featured several times on *America's Most Wanted* but managed to elude the cops for eighteen months before being captured in Canada.

Sarah was capable of being gone a long time. "She's a survivor and knows how to make friends," Larry Sells, the man who prosecuted Sarah, told a reporter at the beginning of December.

Tips kept rolling in that had Sarah dancing at strip joints to fund her freedom. "We have discovered there are a lot of women around the country who are dancers and look a lot like Sarah," an exasperated Deputy U.S. Marshal Rob Jackson, based in the Indianapolis office, said that same week.

It was contagious, this unstated panic that law enforcement just might lose this one. A double murderer had vanished. Even the relentless Ryan Harmon, the Indiana State Police sergeant assigned to the U.S. Marshals' office, was wondering where Sarah was. He was already checking online for plane ticket prices to Florida. He would drop by to see Bonnie Prosser in Bradenton. After all, in her talks with Sarah's friend and fellow inmate Anthony Kelly,* Bonnie was already conspiring to secure her daughter a false ID to further enable her escape.

Bonnie, in fact, was panicked. She was picking up information from some of those who knew Sarah at Rockville that she was running around, low-lifing it at titty bars around Indianapolis, cavorting with a criminal element. And then the claim on *America's Most Wanted* that she was turning tricks for cocaine. Well, it was all too much.

Once again, Anthony Kelly,* the inmate who had agreed to try to help get Sarah into custody, placed a call to Bonnie from his cell phone inside his cell. He let Bonnie fret.

"If we don't hear anything, that's good news," Bonnie said, her raspy voice hitching, a tic of emotion. "Maybe [the news that Sarah was on the street] was a bunch of shit. Until we hear something concrete, we just hope she's not in Indiana. The only time I heard from her was when she first got out, a day or so after . . . What's happened from that point forward, I don't know."

And when talk turned to Sarah's so-called friends from Rockville, Bonnie was wise: "Those people will turn her in quick as shit, especially when there's money involved."

———

Sarah was actually in no such trouble. Returning to Chicago in early December from a two-week break in and around Lafayette, Indiana, with Tom, she once again settled into her work routine. Her days at the Sciortino Group were coming to an end that month. The holidays were always a time to relax, the weather was getting to be Midwest-style nasty cold, and some days construction work couldn't be done. Besides, over her break, she and Tom had decided that Sarah would move to an apartment in Lafayette, and in addition to her job for the Sciortino Group, she would work part-time for Tom's trucking company, GC3 Logistics. Her work would pay the rent and more. Tom had already found the apartment, and things were moving fast.

It was a sublet from a young man who was graduating from Purdue in December, and Tom had secured it. Initially, the place was going to be a layover pad for himself, as he was spending a lot of time doing business in the area. But he thought Sarah could use it full-time, and he could stay on an as-wanted basis. The lease was signed by Welch's business partner, Doug Skoog.

"He thought I was one of [Tom's] girlfriends who needed [a place] . . . Doug didn't have a clue," Sarah said.

Sarah would continue to be Tom's clandestine lover, and she was fine with that. She loved him and told him so repeatedly. GC3 worked out of a couple of spaces in the Lafayette area, and having Sarah nearby, and his wife tucked away with her career in Avon, would serve Welch just about right.

"Tom wanted me close . . . I knew I was just going to be a mistress," Sarah said. She was finding bookkeeping mistakes in the GC3 accounts as soon as she began looking at them via the QuickBooks software that Tom had put on her laptop.

"He needed me to work at his company. I had already started working on his books and reconciling his books and he had lost money."

She was amazed at how it was all falling together, as if it were meant to be. At this rate, she would never be found. Her lip augmentation was only the beginning of her change of appearance. She had an appointment on December 22, just a week or so away, when she would return to Chicago for one last time to get some more cosmetic surgery: "A nose job and then get some permanent eyeliner makeup to always accentuate my eyes," she said.

The move to Indiana from Chicago was like walking through the gate and into her new life—a new face, a good job, a lover. It was the perfect existence of averageness, of a random life led by millions of other Americans. And it was all coming from the cover of this man she had met randomly.

"I had to go on faith," Sarah said. When she first met Welch in the seedy motel in Indianapolis, "I'm thinking 'OK, so this guy will help me out for a couple weeks, put me up, and then maybe hook me up with a job some place and then be OK.' Basically what [he] got in return was my company, my sex, companionship, whatever. And when it developed into more of a relationship, then he said, 'Could you do this for the rest of your life?' And I thought, 'Look I'm living on borrowed time anyway so if this is what I have to do then yes, absolutely, why not?'"

She was aware that the situation was putting a strain on Welch, yet he was persisting in making things right for her. She had considered disappearing in Chicago.

"I loved him," she said. "I didn't want to hurt him or anything like that, but I also knew that it was causing problems in his life, but he wasn't willing to let me go and I thought maybe I needed to make that decision for him. But in the beginning after that first date the fact that once he got past me being in Cincinnati, you know we had our fun and whatever. He's not going to turn me in because if he turns me in, I've got on him just as much as he has on me, I mean he's got just as much if not more to lose and he knows that. We talked about it, and he was like you know what happens if . . . We went through lots of different scenarios. I told him that if I ever get caught I wouldn't implicate him, you know, I wouldn't get him in trouble or anything like that . . . and I told him don't cross me. If you don't want to do this anymore just tell me . . . that's not a problem, I'll go."

She only asked that he not back out by turning her in. He gave no indication of having any such thought.

———

At the end of each year, *America's Most Wanted* does a roundup of hard-to-nab convicts, escapees, and bad guys on the run. It's a studio job of cobbled-together clips and interviews from previous segments, broadcast when viewership is traditionally low. Holidays wreak havoc on bad news, with most people spirited enough to avoid the downer of crime.

Sarah was the most wanted woman in the United States. On December 20, the roundup show ran with Sarah's case at number five out of fifteen hard-to-solve cases featured that evening. The five-minute segment was a video rehash of Sarah strumming her guitar, footage of Larry Sells poring over the crime file at police headquarters, and Jamie Long again informing the world that she considered Sarah her wife.

"She has the ability to seduce others to commit atrocious acts," Sells said, a refrain of his previous Charles Manson comments.

The episode offered no new photos and repeated the fabled "sex for cocaine" notion. It was unimaginative and halfhearted, almost betraying a feeling that this was becoming a lost cause.

"I can't figure out why we haven't caught this woman yet," Walsh said in closing. "But the U.S. Marshals are at our hotline tonight and they're ready to roll on your tips."

But the man who had surrendered any semblance of a normal life in search of Sarah was actually giving back to his family some of the time he had devoted to the case. Ryan Harmon decided that night to take the family to visit his grandparents in Constantine, Michigan, just north of the Indiana border.

———

As a tactical officer for the Chicago Police Department, Mike Grzyb was accustomed to long, dull nights. December 20 was one of them, a wickedly frigid evening at 16 degrees with some snow.

The thirty-two-year-old father of a two-year-old was one of six officers on the team that evening. The Christmas season gives law enforcement two scenarios, and neither is good. One is a dull shift in which nothing interesting happens at all. Another is a night filled with angry families together for the first time in months, or years. Grzyb liked shots-fired calls, something with some action. But nothing like that was going down on that evening.

Around 10 p.m., a call came across the radio at the headquarters on North Clark Street. A tipster advised that a woman who was profiled on *America's Most Wanted* a few minutes ago was living at 2204 West Farwell, apartment 3-E, in Rogers Park. Her name was Ashley Thompson, the male caller said. But the TV show called her Sarah, he said. He knew her only as Ashley. Then he hung up before any more information could be gleaned. But it was specific enough to warrant a visit.

Grzyb and two other cops were wrapping up a traffic stop at a gas station on the corner of Howard and Sheridan, maybe two miles away from the place on Farwell. They were being backed up by another car. Everyone was there, so they all decided to take a run over to follow up on the tip.

Most of the time, when Grzyb and his crew received warrant tips, they were locals—a girlfriend ratting out her estranged boyfriend or a lingering suspect from a crime from days or weeks previous.

Grzyb had no idea who had been profiled on *AMW* that evening, nor was he interested in who Sarah was.

One more tip, maybe good, probably not good. This was no big deal, most of them figured. In fact, they were wondering aloud why the call came to the department rather than the prolific *AMW* tip line.

The aging three-story apartment building was what was referred to as a courtyard building, in that it was defined by an open space in the front. Grzyb walked up to the door with two other officers and looked: Ashley Thompson, 3-E. He rang the bell to apartment 1-D. It almost always worked; either the tenant just rang them in or asked who it was, then let them in. This time, the tenant just rang them in. They had the element of a surprise knock on 3-E.

The three other officers stayed outside, near the back of the horseshoe-shaped building. Someone could skirt out the back if no one was watching, and Sarah's apartment had a back door that opened onto an alley where the Dumpster was.

The officers stood outside Sarah's door and looked at each other briefly before Grzyb knocked, once.

"Maintenance," he said, a hopefully harmless identifier.

Sarah opened the door, barefoot, wearing a T-shirt and gray sweatpants. Her hair, dyed red, was somewhat askew, and she looked sleepy, as if she were getting ready to retire.

They told her they were the police. They held out their badges.

"Do you have any identification?" Grzyb asked.

"I don't, no," Sarah said, somewhat puzzled. She was

caught off guard and had no defense, no plausible alibi. All these weeks of freedom and she had never prepared for a showdown in her own apartment.

"I do have a copy of my cable bill," she said. But that wasn't going to cut it.

"Who are you, what's your real name?" Grzyb probed. He was as confused as Sarah appeared to be. What did he have here?

They stood, looking around. Boxes, packed and taped, were stacked in the small living room. In the bedroom, a full-sized suitcase and a backpack were both full and ready to go. On the counter lay two estimates for rhinoplasty from two different local surgeons. They all looked at her.

Silence.

"OK, you guys finally got me," Sarah said with a sigh.

"We got you for what?" one of the officers asked, somewhat perplexed. They all stood at the door, looking at each other. The cops all knew there was something about her being a fugitive, but none of them knew she was the most wanted woman in America. They certainly didn't know she was on the run from a life sentence for a double homicide; they discovered that only when they got her into the car and ran her name and Social Security number, which she readily provided.

"We didn't even have our guns drawn," Grzyb says.

Sarah later said she was resigned to her capture even before they arrived, but at the moment, facing Grzyb, "I just knew it was time to go. I'd always known there was going to come a day."

The drive back to the station, first on Clark, then downtown to the main jail in Cook County, was quiet, Sarah looking out the window at a world she would never see again. She was quiet until they finally got to the Cook County Jail, on North California Avenue. Then, bolstered with a couple of cigarettes, she talked.

She told them of drinking with some of their colleagues with the Chicago Police Department, some of whom gladly bought her drinks.

Grzyb asked her what she had been doing for a living.

"Working for a local construction company," Sarah said proudly. "I pay my rent; I work every day."

They found three cell phones in her backpack, and Grzyb asked if she called anyone or had any help. She didn't rat out her benefactor, Tom Welch.

"I make cell phone calls but drive four hours away so they can't trace where I am," she said.

Finally, after a lot of talk, she looked at her captors.

"So you guys are just Chicago police?" she asked. Sarah did not mask her disappointment.

"It was like we let her down, as if she deserved something much better," Grzyb says. "I got the impression she wanted flak-jacketed troopers with helicopters and smoke grenades."

Instead she was ratted out by an anonymous caller, someone who failed to even provide enough details to grab the $25,000, tax-free reward. Some, including Grzyb, feel it could well have been her employer, Sam Sciortino, who had only been trying to do the right thing in employing what he thought was a woman in need. Instead, he unwittingly abetted an escaped felon. Sciortino denies even knowing Ashley Thompson or Sarah Pender. The reward remains in the hands of justice.

————

Ryan Harmon was driving his family home from Constantine, Michigan, at around 11:25 p.m. when he got the call from the Chicago Police Department. The Harmons had been visiting Ryan's grandparents for Christmas. But he had taken some time off from his obsessive tracking of Sarah—the very thing he almost refused to do weeks before when *America's Most Wanted* simply wanted some camera time from him—and it had all gone down without him.

Curiously, his first instinct was to call Rick Hull, the man with whom Sarah committed the crime. Hull had been honorable, Harmon thought, and was actually concerned for Sarah's well-being rather than making his cooperation with the cops' hunt a self-serving legal notch. "I told Rick before I told anybody about this," Harmon says. "I told him that night and made sure that he didn't tell anyone. The next day he texted me."

It was a text of relief.

————

Even in the ranks of *America's Most Wanted*, hope had waned.

"We had almost given up at that point," says Jenna

Griffiths, *AMW* producer. For every other airing besides
the one on December 20, she had been in the studio,
watching hopefully as tips came in. Those tips were sent
immediately to Harmon. But until now, when she was
least expecting it and preparing to drive home to her parents' house in Connecticut from her place in New York,
nothing had worked out.

She didn't sleep the rest of the night.

———————

Harmon arrived home around 1 a.m., then got back up at
6 a.m. and made the three-hour drive to Chicago and went
straight to the downtown Cook County Jail, where Sarah
had been transferred for processing and arraignment.

At the jail, it was the cat meeting the mouse. They
came together in a meeting room, Sarah bound hand
and foot. The two shook hands amid the clicking of her
shackles.

"Glad to meet you," Sarah said. "Wow, you're better
looking in person than you are on TV."

"It's not going to work, Sarah," Harmon replied.

"That's cold," Sarah said, smiling slightly.

Harmon's goal was to have Sarah waive extradition,
which she agreed to do. The two sat at a large conference
table, two female guards by the door. For an hour, they
chatted.

"It was surreal," Harmon says. "She had this smirk
on her face, and she was larger than I thought she would
be. I was chasing a woman that I had never met, and

had only seen portfolio pictures of. Her hair was kind of in a bun, and she had glasses. And as we spoke, it would move from laughter and then, occasionally, two tears would drop out of her eyes, like she knew it was over.

"First, when I asked about the chase, she would ask questions. Then, when she asked about what might happen to her from here on, I told her I had no bearing on that. Then she was disappointed. I think she just wanted to talk about her time on the run."

Which was fine with him. "This was like a game film for me. I was as curious about where she had been as she was ready to tell me."

Sarah told him she had been looking forward to spending Christmas in Florida with her family.

"It was so clear that she was disappointed about that," Harmon says. Sarah asked to speak to her mom and dad, via phone, which Harmon made happen. Then he left to check on apartment 3-E in Rogers Park.

Harmon was accompanied by Willard Plank, chief investigator of internal affairs at the Indiana Department of Correction, and they met two Chicago police detectives at the apartment. For Harmon, it was another look at the quarry's life, the way his prey made her nest. It also told him just what kind of prize he was chasing.

"The first thing I realized was that she was trying to piece together a life," he says. "It was a piecemeal apartment. Nothing matched. The dishes were all mixed, like she went to secondhand stores and garage sales to get them. She had a guitar, which she wanted me to grab and give to the Department of Correction so someone there can use it. She had been living a life of grab and go. She had a stack of porn DVDs, lesbian porn, in the kitchen next to the cereal box. She had a whole bunch of soaps, like girls like, lined up around the bathtub. You could tell she liked baths. And she had a lot of junk jewelry. It was like she was trying to get back all that she had lost while she was in prison. She could never have nice soap in there, and this wasn't even that nice, but it was better than she had had for the last eight years."

One more thing he noticed was her key ring.

"She had keys, a huge key ring, and I had no idea what these keys might go to," Harmon says. "I started looking at these keys. Those are the kinds of things that go with someone who has a life of some sort, something going on. I started to realize that she was really trying to take over somebody's life, and that somebody was herself. She had a new life; this guy was going to help her. It was really going to happen. That's what those keys meant."

Harmon spotted her Bible, then her backpack, which contained three cell phones, a laptop that Tom Welch had bought her, and a stack of papers. Harmon took the backpack back to his hotel room to examine.

"And that night, as if the day hadn't been enough, it had notes in there of different ways to kill and die, things about blowing heads off people—crazy, sick stuff she had printed out from the Internet that I never expected."

Sarah waived her right to challenge extradition, and on a sunny December 22, and with Plank at the wheel, Harmon took a seat next to her in the backseat of a Ford Taurus for the drive back to the Indiana Women's Prison in downtown Indianapolis. The car hadn't gone three miles before Sarah was describing her escape to Harmon.

During the ride back to Indianapolis, Sarah spilled to Harmon about Tom Welch, the Sciortino Group, her escape, her contacts on the outside. And looking at her in her yellow Purdue hoodie sweatshirt, her oversize thick-framed glasses, and her poufed-up red hair, Harmon was feeling some satisfaction, even though he hadn't been the one to put the cuffs on her. It was his pursuit, his hard work, his late nights and early mornings that shut down Sarah's avenues for money and kept her friends from helping her. But fate —with a dash of fortitude and a big splash of luck—had somehow allowed her to avoid detection, despite her failure to really hide out, for 136 days.

"I always felt there was a bridge that time laid out for her to get where she was that night in Chicago," Harmon says. "She found her lottery ticket with Welch when she was first out. The smart thing for her to do would have been to cut ties with him, though. But she was going to move to Lafayette and settle in. She really did trust this guy."

At the edge of Indianapolis, the Taurus was met by

two state police cars. They led the car the rest of the way to the prison, rooftop emergency lights spinning.

As they closed in on the prison, where Sarah knew she would be locked down for the foreseeable future, stuck in solitary confinement, she started to cry.

Harmon noticed and pulled his iPod and headphones from his jacket and offered them to her.

She sniffled, smiled, and took the device, plugging in the headphones and looking through Harmon's musical taste. Finding something close to what she liked, she pressed play, closed her eyes, and after listening for a minute, began to sing along to the music buzzing into her head, Alanis Morissette's "All I Really Want":

> *And all I really want is some patience*
> *A way to calm the angry voice*

The cars pulled up to find a substantial media stakeout, with satellite trucks and notebook-holding reporters awaiting the arrival of this infamous escapee, who had made a mockery of the state's correctional system by simply walking out of prison. The state had made sure the media knew of Sarah's arrest and return. A cadre of correction officials stood among the crowd, hoping to bask in the glory of her capture.

Harmon got out of the car, walked around the back as plumes of exhaust wrapped his legs, and opened the other door for Sarah. For a second, they looked at each other, standing face-to-face.

Her wrists were bound, but she moved toward him as

correctional officers came forward to take her to her cell. Harmon, sensing her need for some connection, perhaps something that would formally mark the end, moved to meet her, hugging her in a brief embrace.

Then, Sarah was whisked away, her last walk outside prison walls kissed by the icy December air.

CHAPTER 11

Although Scott Spitler, the lowly guard who sneaked Sarah Pender out of Rockville Correctional Facility, and Jamie Long, who picked up Sarah in the prison parking lot and secured her in a safe house, were sent to prison for their deeds, Tom Welch was never charged.

The facts were presented to the Marion County district attorney's office by Ryan Harmon, with the agreement of Welch's counsel, in early 2009. Since Welch had no prior record, and the crime he committed—aiding a fugitive—was a low felony, it is unlikely he would have received any jail time.

"It would have been a suspended sentence, probably," Harmon says. "I asked that we maybe make [Welch] pay some of the cost of catching Sarah."

That was also a no-go, Harmon says, adding that

Welch had already agreed, informally, to plead guilty to a misdemeanor. But the DA's office declined to prosecute.

"The prosecutor was just not interested," Harmon says, and he left it at that. He had, after all, done his job and more. He had pressured Sarah Pender to the point that she could never rest. His pressure finally forced an error, perhaps not directly, but at least it made enough people aware of the case, including *America's Most Wanted*, that it prompted her capture.

For this book, Marion County prosecutor Carl Brizzi and his representatives declined to address any reasons they might have for failing to press charges on Welch.

Brizzi was first elected in 2002 and reelected in 2006. The father of four children, Brizzi has received plenty of accolades over the years, named an outstanding young alumnus from Valparaiso University School of Law as well as landing on the list of the top fifty most influential people in Indiana politics by *Howey Politics Indiana*, a state capitol news report.

But when the Welch involvement in the state's biggest prison escape in years hit his desk, Brizzi had, perhaps, other issues on his mind.

In January 2010, it was discovered that Brizzi had accepted $29,000 in campaign donations from the millionaire father of Paula Willoughby, a convicted murderer who was released eighteen years into a one-hundred-and-ten-year sentence for plotting to have her husband killed.

Brizzi accepted the campaign money after negotiations for the release of Willoughby had begun. Brizzi also received money from lawyers in the law firm representing Willoughby. In fact, the convict's primary lawyer, Jennifer Lukemeyer, sponsored a fund-raiser for Brizzi at one point.

Brizzi denied any impropriety and, as the story was unfolding, returned the money he had received from Willoughby's father.

An interesting twist to the scenario is that Lukemeyer also represented Richard Hull in his appeals process. But Hull did not receive any of the favors Willoughby did.

Brizzi also faced trouble regarding his ties to Indianapolis businessman Timothy S. Durham, who was a generous contributor to high-profile state and local Republicans, including Brizzi. Federal officials suspect Durham of running a Ponzi scheme at one of his companies, Fair Finance, in Akron, Ohio, and defrauding investors, but as of July 2010 no charges had been brought. Brizzi invested in a Los Angeles movie company with deep connections to Durham. Shortly before the investigation broke, Brizzi also agreed to serve on the board of Fair Finance but changed his mind after Durham told him a newspaper was working on an investigative story about the company.

On the heels of this, all of which began a year after Sarah Pender was back behind bars, there were calls for Brizzi to vacate his office. Politically, it was a black eye for a man who many people apparently already disliked.

Further, it appeared that in addition to a somewhat flimsy corrections system, there was also the appearance of justice for sale in the state's largest city.

———

Meanwhile, Department of Correction spokesman Doug Garrison vowed that the state would find anyone who might have assisted Sarah during her time on the run.

"There's an ongoing investigation as to who may have helped her while she was out of prison, who may have provided her support or money," Garrison said, shortly after Sarah was captured. He declined to ever again speak to anyone about the capture despite being pressed on the issue.

Scott Spitler, the Rockville Correctional Facility guard who had sex with Sarah and smuggled her out of the prison, was caught by a TV crew during a court appearance in January, three weeks after Sarah's arrest.

"Are you sorry?" a news reporter asked Spitler as he was loaded into a white van after his court date.

Spitler nodded, not looking at the reporter or the microphone stuck in his face.

"Scott, what did you think about Sarah getting caught?" the reporter asked.

"It's a good thing," Spitler replied, again, looking straight ahead.

———

Harmon had chased Sarah for so long. Hearing from her of Welch and how he had aided her, slept with her, and kept her whereabouts a secret made meeting Welch a worthwhile endeavor for Harmon.

It was one more way to put the whole case to bed. For him, there were more escapes from Indiana prisons, more fugitives to catch. During a week of vacation after Sarah's return to prison, Harmon pondered what she had told him, the story about being sheltered by this man: the casinos, the jobs, and the plan to move to Lafayette, just an hour north of Indianapolis, to be his mistress.

One evening in early January, Harmon called Welch at home.

"His wife answered, and he came on the line. I told him who I was, and fifteen minutes later, his attorney called me and asked me what this was all about," Harmon says. "I told him he was a witness. And I was asked to come down to his office and meet with Welch and ask questions."

The lawyer, Andy Borland, and Welch met with Harmon on January 8, 2009, at Borland's office in central Indianapolis.

Welch had arranged all of his receipts in a notebook, making the tracking of Sarah's whereabouts during her flight a simple task.

"Tom, you can just start me at the beginning," Harmon told him, as the trio gathered around a conference table.

"The first time I met her, we were at the hotel there at Speedway," Welch began. "I think it was August, early August."

Harmon interrupted to make sure Welch didn't try to play him or get the facts lost in some sort of fabrication. He needed hard times and facts. The detective had already deduced the date from his conversations with Sarah. But these dates had to add up.

"She escaped August 4, which was a Monday," Harmon said. "Would you say it was within that week?"

"Well, last night I kinda went through my credit cards and it was August 6 that I met her there at the hotel, the Budget Inn, here it says right here in Indianapolis," Welch said. His memory was enhanced by his record keeping over the course of the interview.

"You hadn't met her before?" said Harmon. He knew the meeting came through a thinly veiled prostitution solicitation. But he wanted to see how Welch would play it.

"I didn't know her from Abraham Lincoln," Welch said with some small degree of pride. "And ah, it was just a situation where we started talking and—"

"You just didn't randomly show up?" Harmon interjected, in mock astonishment, hinting that Welch was covering something up. He knew he was. Would Welch tell the truth?

"No, ah, well what happened was, I had—" Welch stammered. He paused a couple of seconds, time in which a cornered man savors his secret before disclosure. "I'm embarrassed to say this but I have a sexual addiction of pornography and strip joints," Welch said. "And I mean, unfortunately, I can take you to four or five strip joints and they know me by name and I have a reserved seat. And I'm working on it, I'm going to get help."

Welch offered the testimony of a man scared straight, and he was believable in his statement of redemption. His voice became low, solicitous.

"No matter what happens, my life is better and I can quit lying to my wife, I can quit cheating . . . whatever happens, today is a better day for me than it was yesterday."

For more than two hours, Harmon and Welch discussed Welch's life, Sarah's trail, and the eccentric blend of the independently wealthy fiftysomething man and the escaped murderess.

"God, this is embarrassing, but it is what it is," Welch said as he began telling of his meeting with Sarah through the stripper Thea Fisher. "We just kind of hit it off."

From the moment of being introduced straight through the next three days, "it was 80 percent of the time sex," Welch said. "Just anything, everything, whatever you wanted . . ."

Welch detailed his left turn into sex addiction, which included strip-club visits five nights a week. He blamed a traveling wife, an early semi-retirement, plenty of cash, and a brush with death two decades previous.

"I'm bored . . . so I started I think living in the strip joints; you know, I've always had the propensity without a doubt. I might stop in there two, three times a day: over the last five years it might be five days a week. I might even eat dinner there.

"And since this happened," he continued, referring to his possible criminal case regarding sheltering a fugitive, "I really tried to reflect, 'What makes me do this?' It's like anything else, like when Clinton got caught it was 'Well. I'm sorry.' Well, are you sorry or are you sorry 'cause you got caught? And I've really had to try to think through this. . . . 18, 19 years ago, um, I have a disease. I don't know if you know what myasthenia gravis is but it's like muscular dystrophy where most generally you're in a wheelchair."

Welch told a story of spending eighty-nine days in intensive care at the age of thirty-two for the malady, receiving last rites and undergoing numerous surgeries. An operation saved his life, he said, but it also left him with a vigor for living that transcended a moral code.

"I don't want to be a person at sixty where you say 'What was it like to jump out of a plane?' I did that," Welch said.

Harmon was unmoved. He directed him back to the subject at hand. He was not there to hear excuses for criminal behavior from a man who had made his job difficult.

Welch told Harmon of Sarah's move to Chicago, of one romantic day at Navy Pier.

"We're not hiding anymore," Welch told Harmon. "We're dating. We're dating . . . It's like, well, 'Let's go down to Navy Pier, I've never been there,' so I was like, 'Well, let's go.' So that's what we did."

Welch described handing off his American Express Gold Business card to Sarah when the couple was out, and she would sign the bill if he were, say, around the corner or in another part of whatever store they were in.

"Let's say we could have been together and she was

buying a top and I was over there; she took it and then signed the receipt," Welch explained. "She was getting toothbrushes, deodorant, all kinds of stuff, and of course, I was always like, 'Here, I'll put that on my credit card' because it was my company credit card."

Welch also admitted that he rented the furniture and a television set for her Chicago apartment, but "she was going to pay me back."

Welch told Harmon that he had planned to have Sarah work on his books to find errors. Welch explained to Harmon that he was having some trouble tracking money and that Sarah had looked his books over. And he had secured her an apartment in Lafayette, where his business was located, north of Indianapolis.

"That's the reason she was trying to help me and balance the books, because the girl that we had had screwed up everything," Welch said, almost rationalizing his pending employment offer to Sarah. "So, what [that] meant was I was going to lease this apartment for however many and then go up there and stay a few days a week and all that, and that's not to say she wouldn't stay up there. I mean, she definitely would have."

But the last time he saw her was at a hotel in Lebanon, Indiana, where the two met, and he handed off some of his data on QuickBooks "so she could plug in Quick-Books so we could work. I was going to have her help me. And we could do that virtual, whatever. That was the last time I saw her."

Near the end of the conversation, Harmon asked how he could have been so oblivious to the risk he posed to himself by hanging out with a convicted double murderer.

"Most guys would look into it a little bit," Harmon said. "This gal was on national TV for weeks."

"Basically, my whole routine is I watch sports and read the sports page and that's about it," Welch replied. "I have been thinking about that. My wife is like, 'What the fuck, you're putting yourself at risk. She could have killed you or me, or whatever.'

"You know, I can't explain it other than the sex was . . . she knew that was my Achilles' heel. Not just knew it but knew it and used it. I don't know if when in prison she learned psychology, hypnosis, I don't know. 'Cause she trances you. She does."

Sarah's legacy of manipulation, mind games, and an almost uncanny ability to get others to help her or do what she wants had ensnared Welch, it was clear. He admitted it, and now Harmon had heard it firsthand. Before, it was a lot of words tossed around and reputation. Welch may be weak, but who better to manipulate?

As the session wound down, Welch had a chance to ask a question.

"How did she get caught?"

Now it was Harmon's chance to talk. He was an expert listener, and as such, his impressions of the entire episode were like a book in his mind, flipping pages constantly. He first wanted to explain how she got caught.

"There was a neighbor at the apartment complex that was watching *America's Most Wanted* that night, that Saturday night," Harmon explained simply to the two men in the office listening. But he had more to say, and it came out in a flood. He spoke of his investigation that had gone cold in the days before December 20, when Sarah was caught.

"It was very quiet, hauntingly very quiet," Harmon said, and Welch and Borland sat intently listening. It was as if, finally, Harmon got to tell his own little story, and he commanded his audience and began to weave his own experience with Sarah Pender.

"As it got quieter and quieter and the light got brighter and brighter in her story, *People* magazine was going to do something. I wanted to turn the lamp brighter on her, as bright as I could turn it and as long as I could turn it. Why? Because I think it's going to bed her down, and she's not going to be able to move as much. This guy called at about 11:20 or 30, and my phone rings. It's the marshals in the studio, and they're like, hey, we have Chicago PD on the phone and they have penned her, and they put me in. The neighbor called the local precinct, not the studio, and said, 'Hey I think my neighbor might have been on *America's Most Wanted*. Here's her apartment.'

"The precinct sent two officers, they are undercover guys, they dress bummy and shit like that, but they are in a squad car that is unmarked. They do vice and ghetto alley shit, sneak and peeks. Two guys that are partners, at the end of their shift, this is going to be some bullshit lead, some nutcase, but you got to as a cop check it out. Out of 1,000 different calls, who'd ever guess that this would be the call? They went to the door, she opened it

up, they said, 'Are you Ashley Thompson?' and they said
that within seconds she said, 'I'm the one you are looking for, I'm Sarah Pender,' then turned herself around.
They were like 'OK.' Well, this neighbor never did leave
his name. Never did tell anybody. I have no idea who
he is, and as you can see, right before Christmas he
could have got $25,000 no tax, government reward. . . .
Now, I know you are emotionally connected to her,
going back to October or whatever, but if we had met
this way, with Andy [Borland, Welch's lawyer], and we
were going up there to get her, I would have dropped that
[$25,000] in your lap. That's to motivate people. But the
thing is, it may have worked.

"The thing for the ex-offenders within the first couple
of days, Peggy [Darlington] is the one that was helping
her move around until she met you. Linny [Fisher], she
was on parole from Rockville, we were watching her
tight. At one point, we were in this ex-offender world,
and there's nothing tighter than this underground world
of these dyke Rockville ex-offenders. They are tight, and
they wouldn't talk, and Linny was the same way. So, that
reward money to these parolees is a lot but it wasn't
working. Sarah wasn't reaching out to family, because I
was all up in that world, too, ten different ways, and she
knew we were watching her parents and family. So I
knew she was with someone who was taking care of her.
And I like the ending—the fact we got to save taxpayers
money. I'm all about that."

With that, the conversation was over. Harmon left the
law office spent but pleased that he had just been able to

elucidate his own case verbally. The cathartic venting in front of a captive audience that had no leverage to judge him or his efforts was a release. After speaking with Welch, he was also satisfied that he had done his best to catch Sarah, who had proved to be the most elusive of any fugitive he had ever chased.

———————

But Harmon wasn't finished with the case even after sitting down with Welch. The next morning, January 9, he headed to Pendleton Correctional Facility, where Rick Hull was locked up. The two had bonded over their similarities; both were men of large size, both were high school football stars. Both were born and raised in Indiana, and both had a familiarity with the justice system, albeit from different ends of the spectrum. It was Hull that Harmon had called first when he learned that Sarah was captured in Chicago. And it was Harmon that Hull called when his mother passed away in November.

For this occasion, Harmon picked up a foot-long meatball sub at Subway for Hull. Outside food is a treat for any inmate, and it is traded as contraband behind the walls. In this case, though, Hull was treated as a human being because Harmon just felt he was.

"So what is it you want to know about the case?" Hull asked right off the bat.

"Tell me something that no one knows," Harmon replied.

He already knew some things that few others did. Harmon had obtained the results of a 2002 polygraph taken by Hull by the Indianapolis Police Department at the request of Marion County prosecutor Larry Sells.

Among the questions asked were:

Do you know for a fact who shot Tricia [Nordman] and Andrew [Cataldi]?

Hull answered, "Yes."

Were you physically present when Tricia and Andrew were shot?

Hull answered, "No."

On the night of this reported incident, did you shoot Tricia Nordman?

Hull answered, "No."

On the night of this reported incident, did you shoot Andrew Cataldi?

Hull answered, "No."

Hull was given three separate polygraph tests that day. The conclusion of Larry Smith, the polygraph examiner for the police department, jumped off the page at Harmon.

"After careful analysis of this subject's polygraphs, it is the opinion of this examiner that the tested subject told the truth regarding the object of the examination."

Harmon also obtained a statement from Hull taken by Sells in January 2002 that refuted the case presented by the prosecution. In this version, Hull fingered Sarah as the one pulling the trigger. The statement predated Sarah's trial by seven months and Rick's eventual sentence by a year.

"First of all, I did not shoot Drew or Trish," Hull said almost as soon as the tape began rolling for the statement. "I admit what I did do afterwards is a crime, but I did not shoot these two people."

Hull laid out the scenario for the gun purchase for Sells and explained that he and Cataldi had discussed getting a gun for the house, legitimately rather than from the street. Drug dealing had inevitably brought around a criminal element, and with two women in the house, they decided it was a good idea to have something around for protection that would be easy to shoot.

Sarah was the only one in the house without a felony record; therefore, it fell to her to buy the gun, Hull said.

On the day of the purchase, Hull continued, Cataldi handed him $450 in cash for a 12-gauge shotgun. The deer slugs were selected at random, he said.

"I just went over there, there was a bunch of boxes sitting up about eye level with me, and I just grabbed a box," Hull said.

The evening of the murders, Hull said he and Cataldi had a brief argument over the transport of a half pound of pot from Noblesville back to the house on Meikel. It was a small fight between two friends that Hull blamed on Cataldi's increasing irritability and anxiousness brought on by chronic meth use.

"Drew has been up tweaking out on crystal meth; he's been up probably about three weeks," said Hull, who left the house to drive to the liquor store, leaving Cataldi, Nordman, and Sarah alone in the living room.

"I go to the liquor store, get a case of Budweiser and like a fifth of Old Grand-Dad 100 and come back," he said. "Sarah is sitting on the couch, cradling the gun crying and [saying,] 'I didn't mean to do it, I didn't mean to do it,' and I'm, I don't know what to think, I'm sitting here going 'Holy shit, this is not happening, this is just not happening,' 'cause soon as I stepped into the house I smelled gunpowder."

Later, after both he and Sarah had been sentenced and locked away essentially for life, Hull would contradict himself and claim he did the shooting.

———————

It wasn't all adding up for Harmon, which is why he was there at Pendleton, sitting in a cold room feeding Rick Hull a hot sandwich. He wanted some truth.

"You know the funny thing is that I've actually told this story before, to Larry, and he didn't believe it," Hull said.

"Sells?" Harmon asked.

"Yes," Hull said. And he continued. "Ask anybody who knows anything about me, I'm very, very good with a gun. I know how to shoot, I know how to load, and everything else like that. I put the gun together, that I did do."

The reason Sarah was buying the gun, Hull said, was his birthday, which was a week off.

But he carried a Glock on him "at all times . . . that was my normal handgun," and he would not shoot his own roommates in his own house with a shotgun, with deer slugs, which would result in a mess that no one could ever cover up.

"I would definitely use a 9 millimeter before using a deer slug 12-gauge to shoot somebody with," he said.

Hull explained that he did not do one thing, and that was remove the cap from the top of the barrel. Any new shotgun comes with a plastic cap inside the barrel that blocks any dust, dirt, or other detritus from going into the gun and messing up the mechanics.

The cap was found in the body of Andrew Cataldi.

"There's one thing that I didn't forget to do because I didn't plan on going and shooting the gun anytime soon . . . I never did take the cap out.

"It wasn't Sarah that went to the liquor store that night, it was me. I'm being honest with you; I didn't shoot them two."

"So you came back and it was already done?" Harmon asked.

"It was already done," Hull said.

"Why don't you tell me about it?" Harmon said. The story would have no impact on Hull's case. But Harmon was now so engaged in the story, he had to know more. He was smart enough to know that the justice system works, but he had also gained enough savvy over the years to know that sometimes, once in a while, the wrong person gets the blame.

Harmon was aware that Hull had, on several occasions, asserted that it was he who had killed Cataldi and Nordman, most recently during the taping of *America's Most Wanted*.

But Harmon now also knew of Sarah's ways, which were both predatory and intelligent. She had a way to play people that he could hardly believe.

"I came back and Sarah was sitting there on the couch

cradling the gun crying her eyes out," Hull continued. "I looked at her, I smelled the gunpowder and I knew instantly what the hell happened . . . I knew instantly that she shot them.

"I don't think it was intentional. I was like 'What the fuck did you do, kid?' First thing I did was grabbed the goddamn gun 'cause I didn't know what the fuck she was gonna do."

He looked in the other room, and there were his roommates' remains—Andrew on the floor, Tricia sitting upright on a love seat.

"What they said on *America's Most Wanted* didn't make any sense, that we would buy a $500 shotgun for a $150 debt, come on," Hull said.

But why did she shoot them? Harmon wanted to know.

Hull explained that he worked as a bouncer at a downtown beer garden called Ike and Jonesy's, a cop bar and watering hole where young people could get their drink on. The place closed at 2 a.m., and Hull often didn't get back to the house on Meikel until well after 3 a.m.

"I guess Sarah had another guy and Drew and her got into that argument, and he was like 'Man, I'm not gonna let you go cheatin' on my dude anymore' and that's when the trigger was pulled," Hull said. "I don't really truly believe that she planned that."

Harmon listened, asking a few questions, adding that he had not read the case file nor had he formed an opinion as to who was guilty of what. His role was not judicial, nor did he want to assume that role. But he knew that he had to hear what Hull had to tell him. It was something Hull asked of him the night Harmon had called to tell Hull that Sarah had been apprehended in Chicago.

"There's one more thing I want to talk to you about, if you could come by," Hull had asked. Now Harmon was hearing something he hadn't expected.

Hull kept going.

"If I was going to do it, it would have been easy to lure them out to a fishing trip and do it there," he said. But once the deed was done and his friend was dead, Hull said he felt he had little chance at being believed, given his crime-filled background.

"I was a punk ass, high kid and I didn't know what to do. I've been known in Hamilton County for being a dope dealer and everything else like that. Who in the hell are they going to believe, me or this girl who goes to work forty or fifty hours a week at a good company in downtown Indianapolis? I made my bed and now I gotta lie in it. It's that simple. What else can I do? I did everything they wanted me to do. I took their polygraph test, not mine, Marion County's. I took the polygraph and passed it; call Larry, he'll tell you," Hull said, referring to Larry Sells.

And Hull was telling the truth about that. Sells, in fact, had directed the polygraph examiner as to what questions he wanted asked of Hull.

The test came two months after Sells had sat down with Hull and Hull had spelled out how the murders took place, telling him that Sarah pulled the trigger. The story Hull told that day to Sells was almost exactly the same story he had just told Harmon.

Near the end of the interview, Harmon, feeling a chill, zipped up his jacket in the drafty visiting room.

"Getting cold, soft ass?" Hull chided with a smile.

It was time to go. He was almost done.

———

Sarah was now ensconced in an upper-floor cell at the Indiana Women's Prison in solitary confinement and under severe punishment. While most inmates were free to walk the campus of the prison, she was under lockdown.

Harmon had driven over there from Pendleton after the episode with Hull, and it was close to 3 p.m. when he arrived.

He found a woman somewhat different from the one he had accompanied back from Chicago in the cozy backseat of a sedan, the girl he had bought a pumpkin spice latte for at Starbucks during a bathroom stop on her trek back to the prison that was her forever. That kind of luxury was something she would never again have access to.

"She was already going a little crazy from being in solitary," Harmon says.

She explained the whole setup to him almost as soon as they began to talk.

"I don't have a sink, and I can't flush my toilet. I can't open or close my door, I can't turn off my own light. I have a video camera in my room, I can't make phone

calls, I can't have visits. I can't even flush my own toilet.
I'm in like the suicide room . . . the other rooms can't
talk to me. My door has to be closed at all times. If I
come out of my room, all the doors have to be closed.
They are not allowed to talk to me. The Commissioner
said as a direct order, 'If you talk to her you'll get written
up.' The staff can't even talk to me. The staff can only
talk to me if I am asking them for something I need, like
if I need my toilet flushed or I need a pencil sharpener.
Like I could not even get a pencil for like five days; I
think it was more like a week. They ask me if I want ice
or whatever and I can say yes. But other than that there
is no conversation. They cannot talk to me like a normal
person. No conversation outside my immediate needs.
And if it's like a male officer they cannot even speak to
me at all unless there's someone else there. I can't have
my own clothes in there; everyone else has their own
clothes. They have to bring me mine. I just now got my
hygienes. I use to not be able to brush my teeth until I
took a shower and when I take a shower . . . everyone
else can just get let into the shower. I have to get locked
in a cage in the shower. So that I am handcuffed at all
times and I have no contact with the people. If I come
out of my room there has to be three people on the floor.
Two officers and the third has to be a supervisor or a
man. Oh, it's insane.

"I couldn't have any mail at all for like the first week
and a half. And then when they finally came over and
interviewed me . . . They finally let me have a pencil and
paper and they told me I could receive mail right now but

I couldn't order commissary so I have no stamps and envelopes to send out so my parents must think like 'What's going on?' You get what they feed you. . . . which is really bad food."

Sarah had vented about her punishment for the escape. Now Harmon had his chance.

"The convictions are what they are, OK, so, I'm not basing this on any, I haven't reviewed court testimony, I haven't reviewed evidence . . . I've talked with victims' families, Andrew's family specifically. Rick wouldn't have been the one who had done 'em. They were way too sloppy . . . it was something that I think probably Andrew pushed your buttons and it was just heinous . . ."

"So you think I did it?" Sarah asked, somewhat amazed. Harmon's insinuation—that she pulled the trigger—was soft but it had come out of nowhere.

"I think it didn't go down the way, I don't think it went down the way it went down in court," Harmon replied. "I don't think that you just happened to walk in."

Sarah came back with the same story she had told since the beginning, more or less. She and Harmon jousted for another hour.

"I plan shit out, OK, I planned out this escape for a long time," Sarah said. "I would never have dumped two bodies in a Dumpster that anybody can just lift up the lid and look at, OK?"

Harmon kept pushing, noting that Hull had guns, prodding at Sarah, using Hull's lead about rancor between Sarah and Andrew.

"Drew was a piece of shit," Sarah finally admitted.

"You really want to know the truth, yeah, he was. He
used to beat on Trish. He used to physically abuse her . . .
he had anger management problems . . . he put plenty of
holes in my walls . . . I didn't particularly care for Drew,
but it doesn't mean, I didn't hate him or anything."

Harmon took it in, as Sarah's voice began to rise,
clearly agitated. He had chased her and flummoxed her
until she was caught, and this was his last stand, likely
the last time he would ever see her.

Then he played the polygraph card.

"Did investigators ever offer a polygraph to either of
you?" Harmon asked.

"They never offered a polygraph to me. I don't know
if they did to him or not. I think he did take one and he
told me how he passed it."

"He passed it?" Harmon shot back, feigning surprise.
He knew that Hull had passed, and he had Sarah on the
ropes. She had at first said she did not know if Hull had
taken a lie detector test; then she quickly contradicted
herself and said that not only was she aware of it, but she
knew he passed and had told her how he had done so.

"He put a thumbtack in his shoe and as he answered
all the base questions he pushed down so his heart rate
would go up and he would do that with every other question so whether he was lying or not, his heart rate would
reflect that pain."

Sarah told Harmon that Hull had said several times he
was going to kill Cataldi "and he would talk in detail
about how he wanted to do it. . . . First time it was like,
'I'm going to kill him, I'm going to crush his throat.'"

"Wouldn't that be cleaner?" Harmon asked.

"Sure, but you have to remember they are still friends and it's easier to pull the trigger than it is to do hands-on death because then you have to really deal with it," Sarah said. Then she moved to the same story she had told prosecutors eight years before. That Cataldi was taking money and business from Hull, and that formed the crux of the conflict between the longtime friends. She said that one day not long before the murders, Hull had promised her that "when you come home today, I'm going to have this taken care of," hinting that he was going to get rid of Cataldi in some fashion.

But when she came home that day, "nothing had changed, everything was fine, and I'm like 'OK, he was just talking shit.'"

And the night of the murders, she again claimed to have been too afraid to run to the police. She stuck with the same story she had told police; she went out for a walk after Hull instructed her to leave the house, and so she headed for a store to buy cigarettes.

Harmon was not buying it.

"I would be like, not knowing his mind-set, not being sure you can trust him. Why not smoke a joint with someone because at least it's an alibi?" he said.

"But I wasn't thinking that, I wasn't thinking that at all," Sarah replied, her words all coming out in a rush now, and she was rambling in a fashion that made her seem almost unprepared for being accosted by Harmon. After all, he was just in charge of capturing her, right?

"All I was thinking was, I don't know what to do and I am not thinking about protecting myself. I am just thinking about what is going on. Because if I had planned this, I would have planned out to have an alibi.

"After that I kept on telling lies. I kept telling half-truths and half-truths and when I got back and he had done it and I was just like 'Well, he did it. He did it with my gun in my house, so he is gonna get caught. So if I just go along with the program, he's not gonna shoot me and eventually when he gets caught he'll just go down for it. I will probably get something for not reporting the crime and for buying the firearm' but I never thought I would get implicated in the murders because one, I didn't plan 'em to happen and two, it wasn't—there was so much that went on that I wanted to tell him, 'You really need to do this a different way,' but I said 'You don't want to offer him information on how to do this better because that makes me a part of it.' But I was already a part of it—I was just too stupid to see it. I just didn't want to see it. I didn't want to testify against him. You know I figured, I'll just ride it out, whatever. I just couldn't take responsibility for what I had done."

But her escape, she said, was made possible by her own wiles, a form of manipulation that she called charm.

"I mean, I had charm. You know, obviously I had to have some charm to get people to help me but they helped me because they believed in me."

It went on for another forty-five minutes, and then the two stopped, as in a mutual truce. As a parting shot, he asked her if she would be willing to pay back to the state and federal government the costs of chasing her for those 136 days she was on the run.

"If?" Sarah asked hopefully. "If I could get out, if they gave me forty-five years on each charge, forty-five years on a random, concurrently and I could get out in forty-five years? Hell yeah, I would. I would be paying till the end of the days. If I am cooperating here, they should be able to help me out. I mean, I have spent a year here, they want me to testify on other stuff and, you know what, I've already done all this stuff for you, already given all this information, do something for me."

It was over. Harmon stood to go. Sarah, her wrists in the always-present shackles, again stood to hug him. He walked out, and Sarah was escorted back to her cell, forever.

EPILOGUE

It is one of those heartbreaking notes that affect almost anyone who covers violent crime and its horrible hangover. The family of the accused and convicted often suffers every bit as much as the survivors. Who can believe that the child they raised could kill?

Roland Pender, when his daughter was arrested for a double murder in front of his very eyes on that October day in 2000, could barely be contained. He ranted and railed and accused the police of setting her up.

It's a testament to the love of parenthood. And it melts your heart to see.

To this day, Roland Pender cannot believe his beloved daughter is guilty of the crime she was convicted of in 2002. Part of reporting this book involved reaching out to the parents of Sarah Pender, whose escape may or may not have been known in advance by them.

It didn't matter; I was, above all, interested in their daughter's life and how it came down to having to breach the walls of a prison in order to pick up some groceries at Jewel or some toothpaste at Walgreens.

I called Roland a few times before finally reaching him. I left messages on his voice mail, of course, but he never responded. When I finally did reach him, he was blank, barely able to converse about it all. Finally, I e-mailed him some questions, which he agreed to answer.

His response came fairly quickly.

"Steve, Sarah had a normal childhood, ups and downs, you know. Normal. Naïveté got her where she is. Look at her now, talking to you, someone looking to write a book about her conviction of a brutal double shotgun murder of her roommates which were then stuffed in a dumpster. I would give out hope that you might write about how all the main evidence used in her trial was fabricated. The letter is a forgery. The second analysis of the letter was done by the same state lab and not completed until just days before trial. Floyd [Pennington's] testimony was a farce, he had to be reminded of his previous story, as he told something different until Larry corrected him and coached him through it, all the while Sarah's court appointed attorney did nothing, presented no witnesses or any defense at all. There was no bruising on Sarah's shoulder after the murders. Do you think a girl that had not grown up around guns, never went hunting, could aim, and shoot a 12 [gauge] shotgun twice without leaving a mark on herself? Do you think someone as smart as Sarah would plan such a poor plan to get rid of two unwanted fugitive roommates? She stuck around and she helped cover up and clean up, but she did not kill anyone. Larry Sells was running for public office during her trial. Larry was looking to make a name for himself and Sarah was an easy, high profile subject because she was so naive. Indiana justice. I suggest you are barking up the wrong tree. Sarah never changed because she did not do it in the first place. She is a good person, smart in so many ways, and so naive in other ways."

Heartbreaking.

———————

Bonnie Prosser, Sarah's mother, is considerably more circumspect when it comes to the situation. She gladly tells me that Sarah deserved prison—maybe even still does—but that she would at least like to see the case reviewed. Bonnie is a fiftysomething-year-old little fireplug of a woman, with kindly features and round all over. She carries a worried smile that beams a mother's warmth. At the same time, she has some gentle creases that tell of a harder life than that of most people, as if her setbacks have not been profound, but she has never quite mastered the confusion of life. Call it a nervous weariness.

We met over lunch at an Applebee's in Indianapolis one winter day. Bonnie had moved back to the city not long ago, in part so that she could be closer to her daughter and support her. It was no doubt a move made of love, and the fact that she could see Sarah every week was of great consolation to them both.

We talked about Sarah's life as a child, about Bonnie's life, and went through some photos of Sarah growing up.

Some of our conversation revolved around Sarah's current situation, and some around her time as an escaped convict. Bonnie denied ever having a conversation with Sarah during those 136 days. Sarah's version of the story is different, of course, and she said she made one call to her mother on the day she escaped and that her mother was almost delirious with concern.

Bonnie likewise never mentioned the chats with Anthony Kelly,* the inmate to whom she had spoken about getting Sarah a fake ID.

I never pressed the issue. Bonnie had earned the right to tell a little white lie. Her candor on being the mother of a murderer, though, was sad but realistic.

"For them to say she told [Hull] to kill two human beings is beyond my comprehension," Bonnie said. And, like Roland Pender, she doesn't believe it. Sarah's crime was one of omission.

"Sarah did not call the police or leave like she should have, and it made her look just as guilty."

Bonnie's sharp memory, e-mails, and personal interviews helped make this book happen. She was always friendly, and we would talk about her love of playing pool and her travels. Bonnie is an interesting and kind person and deserves respect for how she has stood by her daughter without reserve.

She is hopeful that a book would help her daughter's case for a new trial. She is likely disappointed. But she is one more victim of this tragedy, and victims are often disappointed.

———————

One of the first items I found in my research on Andrew Cataldi was his obituary. It wasn't a flashy obit, as these things go, but it spoke to me enough to realize that he had a family that loved and cherished him. His notice, with the erroneous date of death, ran in several online newspapers around Citrus County, Florida, where his family lived.

Andrew Cataldi, 25, of Indianapolis

Andrew Scott Cataldi, 25, of Indianapolis, Ind., died Friday, Oct. 27, 2000. He was born in Queens, N.Y. on Aug. 19, 1975, to George and Stephanie Cataldi Andrew was a former resident of Inverness. He attended the First Assembly of God in Inverness. He worked in the construction industry. Surviving are his parents, George and Stephanie (Cookie) Cataldi of Inverness; brother, Steven J. Cataldi of Lecanto; sister, Karen A. Dixon of Inverness; and a nephew, Christopher G. Dixon of Inverness. Heinz Funeral Home, Inverness.

I first called Steven Cataldi, a no-nonsense fellow who had little praise for his brother's choice of itinerant lifestyle.

"Andrew never got along with it; he was running away almost immediately," Steven Cataldi told me. "He got kicked out of high school; he was in trouble with the police; he was smoking pot and doing anything else."

Steven's strident dismissal of his brother was tinged with something else, though. Not disdain, but something closer to a closeted regret, as if he had tried a tough-love approach that didn't work. So I pushed, ever so gently, to hopefully gain some insight into the effect the murder had on other members of the family.

"My dad died at sixty-six years old . . . He lost interest in living after Andrew died. He was so full of grief. He kept Andrew's license in his wallet after [Andrew] died. My dad just went away."

Andrew's sister, Karen Dixon, and mother, Cookie, doted on Andrew, and were obviously still mourning even eight years later.

"He was a beautiful boy, six feet two, 170 pounds," Cookie told me. "He was too smart for any school."

She paused long enough to audibly dry her eyes. Her voice became choked almost as soon as she began to speak of her dead son. A woman of faith, she said she had already forgiven her son's murderers.

"I feel no hurt for them," she said. "My son chose a road and he walked down it. I don't hope for them to be hurt, and I don't feel any hate for them. I only wish they would start praying more.

"At his funeral, someone donated $800 so that we could have his ashes taken up in a balloon and have them scattered in the Gulf," Cookie continued. "It was a gift to us, and to him. I still have a picture of that."

She and Karen have lots of pictures of Andrew at home, beaming a wide smile. Never mind for a second the fact that this was a guy who was a criminal. He was also someone's beloved son, brother, friend.

"I'll never forget the night we found out," Karen Dixon told me. "At that time, my ex-husband worked at the sheriff's department, and he saw the notice come through. He came and got me. The cops were on the way to tell my parents, and I said, 'No, I have to do this.'"

Both Karen and Cookie told me that Andrew called Richard Hull both his brother and his bodyguard. They most likely had no idea the two were mostly interested in making a living by selling drugs or that both were devoted users of all substances great and small. Parents and siblings often aren't aware, and if they are, they would prefer not to think about it. Most of the time, such pursuits are the stuff of youth, and the allure wears off with time and experience.

Efforts to reach the family of Tricia Nordman were unsuccessful. She had at least one child, and the fate of that child is unknown. There are many Tricias out there, and that in itself is one more heartbreak. Can you imagine having no one around to mourn your death?

I met with what was left of the family of Richard Hull. That is, Tabitha Hull, his younger sister, the one who was in the car when the police arrested Richard and Sarah that October day in 2000.

Tabitha lives in Noblesville, Indiana, a few blocks from the house in which she grew up. She is twenty-seven years old now, has a couple of children, and is working to get a dental hygienist license. Her road has been hard for some time, due in part to some poor choices she made as a kid. The murder made life hard on her, as it came in the fall of her senior year in high school.

"After it happened, people in school made my life so hard," Tabitha told me in the living room of her small home. It was a tidy place, defined by a giant flat-screen television set that took up most of the living room.

"I never graduated high school at that time," she continued. She dropped out and worked, played, ran with a hard crowd. Her mother died during the time Sarah was on the run.

"Rick and I were very, very close as kids," Tabitha said. "We were often all each other had. He had sports, of course."

She has boxes full of pictures of Rick as a boy growing up, pudgy in wrestler's tights in middle school, puffing a cigarette outside a shiny limo on senior prom night, at football camp as a little boy.

When the box came out—a large shoe box, and the smart money has it there are more where that came from—she pored over pictures just as I did. She was quiet as she looked at them, as if visiting a better time.

Losing Rick was rough, but she moves on with her

own family, her own life. She visits him periodically, but sometimes months go by without her making the sixteen-mile trip to Pendleton Correctional Facility, where Rick is housed.

"Life would be so much better if he were out," she says.

———

Tom Welch understandably didn't want to talk about his time with Sarah. He made a mistake that I am sure he is trying to rectify. We often become better people in the wake of a failure such as his. He has been blessed with a good life by all appearances. Our misdeeds and weaknesses define us as much as our strengths, and he is just a man. Making moral judgments is not the purpose here. We are all flawed and all have things in our lives that are hard to face.

At the same time, it should be remembered that Welch is lucky to be walking free. Sarah's other confederates, Long and Spitler, in particular, are behind bars for a few more years. Prison is a place Welch was lucky to escape.

———

I pulled up to the Pendleton Correctional Facility, and the first thing that struck me was: old school. It was old and older, the main building brownish redbrick with white trim. It is part of a complex that includes a juvenile lockup across the road that has the dubious honor of once hosting John Dillinger.

The adult prison was built in 1923 and looks like it had an upgrade shortly after. Inside, visitors immediately notice the iron just beyond the security apparatus, which includes the usual metal detector but also includes a body scanner.

The bars look exactly like those at a zoo. Primates and carnivores are kept behind those bars. Rick Hull is kept behind these, along with other murderers.

Hull did not look as physically imposing as he had been advertised. His head is disproportionately small on his impressive frame, his brow low, the goatee still there, just as it was on the day he was arrested for murder in 2000. He met me in a private room just off the more public visitation area of Pendleton, which was glassed in but allowed the inmate to still be observed by the guard, who sat at a desk that was raised above the room. It was open air, as well, so anything said was not completely private.

Hull was not concerned at all. He wanted to talk about anything I asked. He smiled frequently, noting his situation with a dismissive shrug, a fuckup's nonchalance. He screwed up, and this is what happened. He laughed when he talked about his life, self-deprecating even. He was a gentleman, actually, despite the swagger he affected when he walked.

"What I would really like to do is have a chance to tell kids who might be headed in the same direction and help them," Hull told me. "It's one thing to read all about it in books, but it's a whole other thing to have lived through it."

He was working toward a degree in psychology, which he felt would put him in that position.

There was more on his situation. "One of the things I have had to come to terms with is that I was a piece of shit," Hull said. "I didn't love my family enough to quit drinking and my druggie ways. It's a harsh realization, and I know now that I have to make amends. It's the only thing I can do. This is a harsh punishment."

He spun off tales of his wild life as a drug dealer, bragging that "anyone who bought steroids in Indiana in the late 1990s, they probably got them through me."

Hull told me that he once had a beach condo in the Bradenton, Florida, area and a boat. He sold steroids and ecstasy. That lasted a few months, until one night he went out for some fun and came back to find his place completely robbed. He drifted back home and continued to sell drugs: steroids, pot, coke, whatever turned a buck. He was successful, he said.

"But I bet in my entire life I made between $7,000 and $8,000 legitimately," Hull said.

Hull talked about Sarah, how he knew her for three months and how they'd spent almost every day of that period together except when she was at work. He again went through his version of the crime, which he had already outlined in depth for both Ryan Harmon and prosecutor Larry Sells. For the state, Hull passed a lie detector test, he noted.

"Ten years later and Sarah has still not taken any responsibility for those murders," Hull said. "It's funny how I can pass a polygraph. And I'm going to spend the rest of my life in prison."

I left after about ninety minutes. Much of what he told

me is included in this book, and he spoke freely, although
it was apparent that ten years in jail and prison had given
him the con's edge, that little nuance of personality that
tells one not to believe everything one is hearing.

———————

There has been another escape in this case, that of the
Indiana Department of Correction.

Sarah's prison break never created the firestorm that
it could or should have. There were no outcries for additional looks at safety and security at the prisons. There
was an internal investigation, of course, and two low-
level corrections officers, Steven Butler and Scott Spitler,
were fired. But Sarah's walk away from the prison in
broad daylight created no curiosity among the citizenry.
No one stood up to ask: "How could this person get out,
and how safe are we from these criminals?"

If Sarah had killed someone after her escape, there
would have been an uproar, and heads would have rolled,
no doubt.

But instead, there was nothing. Aside from the guards,
no one else lost his or her job over Sarah's flight. Edwin
G. Buss, the unfortunate official who took office as commissioner of the Indiana Department of Correction just
three days before Sarah's escape, made $101,000 in 2008,
according to records. Julie Stout, superintendent of Rockville Correctional Facility, kept collecting her $67,968
salary after the escape. Jerry Newlin, considered by some
to be the dean of Rockville, was paid $41,877 in 2008.
They get paid whether they do their jobs well or not.

Stout began her career with the Indiana DOC twenty-five years before the escape, working as a guard and moving up the ranks. Just five months before Sarah's escape, Stout appeared on a panel for the Office of Justice Programs, an arm of the U.S. Department of Justice, and discussed sexual assaults in prisons.

"It is my honor to appear before you, and to report out on the efforts being made at my facility regarding the elimination of sexual victimization at the Rockville Correctional Facility," Stout announced. She spoke of the number of measures she had taken to minimize the risk of sexual misconduct in the prison, of committees formed, and even posters that were slapped up in hopes of reducing the chance of abuse. She addressed mostly offender-on-offender crime rather than the more prevalent guard-on-offender assaults. In her presentation that March 2008 day, she never once mentioned corrections officers or guards.

"To summarize, the Rockville Correctional Facility has taken an active role in preventing sexual assault and in educating staff and offenders regarding our standard of zero tolerance for sexual violence," Stout said. "As employees of the State of Indiana we represent the citizens of Indiana, and we carry out our responsibilities in a professional manner. My staff understands their duties, and continually makes every effort to protect the offender population from threats of sexual victimization."

Her prison was a model, as far as she was concerned. And in the world of institutional oversight, it was, too. Was she completely in the dark about the prolific amount

of sex between guards and inmates that was going on?
Was there no one on the floor—Newlin, perhaps?—who
could let her know that perhaps there were some changes
needed?

Rockville was recommended for reaccreditation after
an audit by the American Correctional Association shortly
before Sarah's escape, passing 100 percent of the 61 man-
datory standards.

————

A year after Sarah's escape, there came more noise from
Rockville. Two lawsuits were filed, one by an inmate
named Jennifer Henry and another by inmate Sovayda
Vasquez. Both alleged they had been sexually assaulted
by guards. In the case of Vasquez, the guard in question,
Roger Heitzman, pleaded guilty to sexual misconduct by
a service provider, a Class C felony.

In Jennifer Henry's case, the guard in question resigned
one week after Henry was released from Rockville.

"I have never seen this kind of thing, where these
cases keep coming out of that prison," says Jeffrey Mc-
Quarry, who is handling both the cases on the plaintiff
side. "I have no idea what they are doing in that prison,
but they need to do something about it."

On the one-year anniversary of Sarah's escape from
Rockville Correctional Facility, news crews came to the
prison to be told of improvements to the security there.
A local television crew was told of new cameras being
added "throughout the entire facility," according to one
fawning news report.

"Somebody's always monitoring the cameras; officers and executive staff have access to the footage," prison flack Pam Ferguson told the reporters.

The story breathlessly proclaimed: "Not only are the prisoners closely monitored, everyone is now searched at the front door, even staffers. They have also added more security to their entrances and exits."

Ferguson went on to describe just how Sarah managed to slip away. "The male staffer in this case fell for some of her tactics and [she] found his weak points and used them to her advantage."

The story continued to say that with all the new security, it was hoped that "Pender will go down in history as Rockville's only escapee."

Which is either a bit of spin, some inept reporting, or a lie being told to reporters by the system.

In 1993, inmates Angel Lucas and Delilah Dunn escaped from Rockville with the help of Lucas's boyfriend, Anthony Morrow. Lucas and Dunn slid through a hole cut by Morrow in a fence at the back of the prison. The two were met by Morrow in a waiting car on the road down the hill, the same road Sarah rode with Jamie Long on her ride to freedom.

Dunn and Lucas were captured within eleven days of their break. Dunn, who was serving eight years on a conspiracy to commit armed robbery charge, was given three more years on an escape charge. Lucas, with about a year left on a five-year forgery charge, was also handed another three years for her escape.

At the time, there was only a single fence with no

razor wire, and the perimeter road that allows guards to check the outside fences had not yet been created.

Then there is the issue of the additional cameras the prison system claims to have put in since Sarah's escape.

I filed an Open Records Request to the prison in October 2009, anticipating some sort of documentation of a security upgrade. In the request, I asked for "vouchers for all repairs, modifications and improvements pertaining to security at Rockville Correctional Facility that amount to over $100,000 between the dates of August 4, 2008, and July 31, 2009."

The response from the Department of Correction came back on December 16, 2009, and reported that "no security improvements in an amount of $100,000 were made during the time period in question."

Good security cameras, even a single camera for your home, can run around $2,000.

It is hard to believe that a system this bumbling and, apparently, dishonest could upgrade security in a major prison for under $100,000.

Therefore, a second request for public information yielded thirty-three pages of invoices that the state had held back from my first query, virtually all of them falling in that time frame I had previously asked for. These showed security upgrades at a cost of more than $500,000 that were approved mostly before Sarah's escape but not completed until after.

The Indiana Department of Correction has escaped, indeed. Taxpayers fund this system, which does the job most of the time. But that is what it is supposed to do.

And when it makes a mistake, someone would expect some honest accounting, not dishonest spin about a new security system that may or may not exist.

In that same request for information, I also asked for "copies of all correspondence related to the August 4, 2008, escape from Rockville Correctional Facility by Sarah Jo Pender. This is to include, but not limited to, summary reports, incident reports, investigative conclusions and recommendations and dismissals of any employees related to the escape."

The Department of Correction refused to provide the information. We will never know who was really remiss at a systemic level in allowing Sarah Pender to walk out of the prison, literally. That itself is a crime for another time.

In addition to the interviews Sarah did for this book, she has made some other public statements.

She saved much vitriol for *America's Most Wanted*. On January 26, 2009, Sarah wrote a letter to John Walsh, the creator of *America's Most Wanted*. In it, she claims that the television show that assisted in her capture was seeking ratings and for that purpose cast her as a "degenerate, dangerous criminal."

"Apparently, justice has no need for the truth, they are merely distant cousins," Sarah wrote.

"I spent nearly eight years attempting in vain to obtain a just sentence for the crimes I committed," Sarah wrote. Again, Sarah claimed that "false testimony and manufactured evidence" were the reasons she received a one-hundred-and-ten-year sentence, mentioning the convict Floyd Pennington's appearance on the stand on behalf of the state.

"The judge denied me a new trial because apparently a convicted felon's testimony is only credible when testifying for the state. When testifying for a defendant, a convicted felon is just a liar. How is that justice?"

She concluded her letter with this: "In the 4 ½ months I was free, I proved I am not the dangerous criminal I've been made out to be. So when do I get justice?"

In early February, Jon Leiberman, the host of the episodes on Sarah, sat down with Sarah for twenty-five minutes.

"My goal was to find out what she was thinking and how she thought she could evade law enforcement," Leiberman says. "I wasn't there to be her friend, because there were a lot of people looking for her for a long time and she felt she deserved to be free. She came off as very manipulative, but when you stand up to her is when you shut her down. If she can't manipulate you, then she will turn off and not be interested in you. If she can't make you believe what she wants you to believe, then she won't waste her time."

From the start of the interview, with Sarah telling producers up front that she wouldn't answer certain questions about her time on the run, it was tense.

"All she wanted to do is relay the idea that the system had done her wrong," Leiberman says. The interview took place at the Indiana Women's Prison. Sarah was led into a room manacled and clad in orange prison scrubs. Her hair, still dyed red but turning to brown, was parted in the middle, and she wore black-framed glasses.

Leiberman asked her where her life had "veered off," and Sarah, with no serious criminal history, was up-front: "I can't say there was any one specific point in my life where I went bad or anything. I think my biggest mistake was getting involved with someone who—well, I was doing drugs, smoking pot every day, you know—so I didn't see drug use as such a bad or a terrible thing, you know, not a big deal and it really should have been because there are a lot of things that go along with you know, drugs and doing drugs that, a lot of consequences you don't see."

She recited the same series of events that ended with the two murders: her fealty to Rick Hull "out of loyalty, fear and sheer stupidity." About the victims, Sarah pointed out that Andrew Cataldi was "a drug dealer, he was also a woman beater, among other things. So, and they were both fugitives."

As far as her reason for escaping, Sarah began to tear up.

"I served the equivalent of twenty-one years on my sentence and that was enough. And after being denied appeal after appeal I decided that I was going to take justice into my own hands and I was going to escape, because I felt like I deserved it. I'd done my time and done my best every day for eight years. And that was enough."

She continued, her voice higher as she got more emotional and weepy.

"And you know what? I'm not proud of some of the things I had to do in order to get out of prison. But I don't regret it. The only thing that I regret is the FBI and the U.S. Marshals and *America's Most Wanted* invading the lives and the homes of my family and friends."

Sarah then echoed much of what she said in the letter to Walsh, asserting her feelings on her trial and the sentence she received and stating that she was a hardworking person while free.

When Leiberman pressed her about the specifics of what she did to get along while she was out, Sarah hedged. She had asked that he not ask about that. Sarah could not control the questions, though.

"I don't want to talk about what I did while I was out," she said. "I didn't commit any crimes and I was just a normal person."

"What kind of life were you living?" Leiberman asked. "How were you living? Were you scared?"

"Like I said, I'm not real interested in airing the stuff that I did or how I did it, you know, that's not of interest."

Finally, she broke, and tears came quickly.

"You know, it's embarrassing to be on this show, it's embarrassing to be on the FBI's Most Wanted List. I don't want that. I'm not looking for fame or some attention at all."

Finally, Leiberman asked her about her capture and relayed what the Chicago police had told him, that she "wanted to get through the holiday."

"I don't want to talk about this anymore," Sarah said

tersely. "I asked you not to ask me questions about that. I gave you my specific wish and you have repeatedly ignored it and that's very disrespectful and I'm gonna go now."

With that, Sarah stood up, the guard that had been seated behind her, off camera, came to her, and Sarah was taken back to her cell.

———————

Sarah next stepped up to a microphone on the anniversary of her escape in 2009. She spoke with the local CBS affiliate in Indianapolis and told a reporter that "everyone thinks of escaping; they just won't admit it." She described her 136 days of freedom as "beautiful, simple," addressing the days only in vague terms. Sarah refused to tell of her leaving the prison, her time with Tom Welch, or the details of her frenzied first forty-eight hours.

"The worst thing I did while I was out was to lie to people about who I was," Sarah said. "I had a job, I had a real job, and, umm, I had a condominium and I took public transportation."

The interviewer asked if she had a message for Jamie Long, the woman who drove the getaway car for Sarah's escape, and Sarah simply relayed, "Thank you for standing up for what you believe in."

Sarah gave another interview to a more hostile local Fox affiliate, which ran mostly video of the *America's Most Wanted* episodes in its episode.

"There's no trust. They don't trust me," she told the

interviewer, mocking her captors, "because they told me I might grow wings and fly away."

Again, she refused to detail her days of freedom.

"When I was on the run, although, of course, I was paranoid about being caught, I was very at peace because I was out in the midst of life. For the four-and-a-half months I was out, I'd run into cops. In fact, I lived in a North Side Chicago neighborhood that a lot of cops live in and, so, pass cops every day. It wasn't the most comfortable feeling and you always wonder. You might hold your breath a little bit."

Presented with the notion that she might just be the manipulative character so many have said she is, perhaps a sociopath, Sarah smiled. "Sociopath? I'm a sociopath? Sociopath has to do with anger and aggression. I'm not angry. I've had a lot of horrible things done to me since I was a small child and I'm not angry."

In one of her last interview letters to me, Sarah spoke of all the terrific things she'd done for humanity.

"Although I have made plenty of choices in my life I'd like to change, I am not ashamed of who I am or who I have ever been in my life," she wrote. "Actions do not capture someone's life. And if they did, you'd never capture all the good, sweet, kind, selfless choices I made on a daily basis."

Sarah went on to speak of a friend who betrayed her by blaming her for an ailing marriage and a coke habit.

This friend, Sarah said, told her that Sarah "made her drink . . . made her do coke . . . made her cheat on her husband. This grown woman. Sound familiar?"

Well, yes, it does. It sounds a lot like the convicted murderer trying again to cast blame in every direction but her own.

Legal doctrine dating back to the 1700s finds that a person who instigates a murder is every bit as culpable as the person who commits it. And yet Sarah Pender, with her own idea of justice, continues to seek a remedy that will never arrive.

Still, she is the woman with the college-level physics acumen who outsmarted a prison system that was just waiting for someone with her smarts to show it how failed its own security measures were. Once free, Sarah fell into the arms of a man who was waiting for her, Tom Welch, who sought sexual fulfillment to wile away his retirement.

And Sarah, never one to miss a chance, latched on to his weakness and rubbed it and nourished it so that she could remain free.

———

Vampires, as lore has it, exist on the essence of others. Sarah Pender was a vampire in the emotional and mental sense.

She thrived on the goodwill and the emotional giving that she could coax from anyone in a position to help her. It is hardly a coincidence that as she grew up and ventured into the world, she was the one with the job, the one to whom others could go when they wanted a word of advice or, as she whirled relentlessly toward her fate as a convicted murderer, some bail money. She made sure that she was the top dog, the queen among the mostly defeated, in order to impose her will.

Sarah's first love, David, was a slow-paced, somewhat aimless individual who was never a match for her energy by most accounts. She dominated him before she left him for a faster-moving crowd.

Richard Hull was a simple, misguided man who by most accounts had a kind heart that was obscured by a criminal nature. Sarah seemed to sense both his bravado and his willingness to carry out a crime. We have seen the results.

She found Floyd Pennington, a man with the afflictions of a sex offender and, as Sarah apparently hoped, a sympathetic ear and an eye on the outside. Was she thinking he knew how to get her out of jail when the two mutually feigned illness in the Marion County Jail? That maneuver had been used before with some success.

Scott Spitler, the guard at Rockville, was ripe for Sarah, a man ready to be compromised in exchange for sex and money.

Jamie Long, her made-in-jail pal, was willing to sacrifice her own freedom to assist Sarah's absurdly self-righteous notion that she had served her time.

Finally, Sarah latched on to Tom Welch, who was manipulated by Sarah's sexual charms wholesale. He never knew what hit him, and Welch was prepared to provide sanctuary forever for Sarah, his mistress.

Ironically, the victims of her manipulation survived, although most ended up in prison. And in the end, none of them came out better for having known Sarah Pender.